DIANA VICTRIX

A NOVEL

BY

FLORENCE CONVERSE

BOSTON AND NEW YORK
HOUGHTON, MIFFLIN AND COMPANY
The Riverside Press, Cambridge
1897

' The last was a strong-minded monadess,
Who dashed amid the infusoria,
Danced high and low, and widely spun and dove,
Till the dizzy others held their breath to see."

EDWARD ROWLAND SILL.

CONTENTS

PRELUDE

BOOK I

"SPINSTERS ALL AND BACHELORS MERRY"

BOOK II

JEANNE'S WINTER

BOOK III

ON THE MOUNTAIN TOP

BOOK IV

"MAN, OH, NOT MEN!"

DIANA VICTRIX

PRELUDE

THE gray clouds drooped above the murky
waters of the lake, and there was a listening hush
upon all things. Jocelin was singing. Under
the bath-house he hung, just above the water; his
attitude was Promethean. Only a growing boy
could have invented and endured so uncomfortable and tortuous a posture; only a growing boy
could have twined his arms and legs among the
rungs of the bath-house ladder as Jocelin's were
twined. They were thin, brown, bare arms and
legs, and they hugged the slimy ladder with a
serpentine tenacity. Jocelin's head was thrown
back as far as the ladder would permit, and his
stomach extended forward in inverse ratio, while
out of his mouth floated the melody, sweet, passionate, solemn, hushing the air to stillness. It
was something from "La Juive," a duct, and
Jocelin sang both parts: —

"O ma fille chérie, O ma fille chérie ! "

The voice thrilled through and through with

paternal anguish, — and Jocelin would be ten years old his next birthday.

It was not a soprano voice; it was low and brimming with sweet music; and in the heart of every note there was a cry, and Jocelin heard the cry, but could not understand. It was a voice to love, and Jocelin loved it, — more than his mother, more than his baby sister and his old colored mammie; more than the beauty of white nights, when there was a silver moon-path wide across the fluttering lake, he loved it. And every one who heard the voice loved it; already Jocelin had begun to know the intoxication of power; already he had begun to thirst for the mysterious exaltation of moments when his fellow-beings, sitting around him, were as statues, while their souls were gathered, passive, into the hollow of his hand. And Jocelin, when he thought upon those wizard moments afterwards, thought with his lips parted and smiling, and the breath coming quickly.

But to-day he sang to the clouds and the lake. And the bath-house above him sent his voice ringing down and out over the water. He liked to sing under the bath-house, because there was so much vibration. In this hour he had forgotten the world and its subtle temptings to ambition, and had lost himself in the delight of his own effort: —

"O ma fille chérie, O ma fille chérie!"

Jocelin's eyes, deep, liquid, brown, were full of a pensive, unseeing sorrow as they gazed into the cloudy distance, and the singing mouth was curved in wistful sadness below the short upper lip. A narrow, long face he had, brown and lean, — this was when you stood in front of him. Seen in profile, Jocelin's prominent feature was his nose; all his other lineaments were swallowed up in this one; like a blank wall it arose from his face, — nay, rather, it was his face, for when, wishing to describe his profile, one had said Jocelin had a nose, there was nothing more to say. The backward droop of his chin was noticeable later.

It was an ancestral nose: from generation to generation it had been handed down through the race, and when, finally, it descended upon Jocelin, neither time nor intermarriage had softened its angles or diminished its size. It was not a hooked nose; there was nothing Jewish in its contour; it was an exaggerated Roman, and sprang forth abruptly, thin and broad as the blade of a carving-knife, between Jocelin's limpid eyes.

There was a portrait of Jocelin's earliest known ancestor in the parlor of the old house in New Orleans, a portrait in profile of a mass of curled hair from which there protruded a nose. Of course one knew at a glance that the hair was a wig, one of those monstrous objects affected by the courtiers of the "Grand Monarque." But that the nose was not likewise an adjunct it took more than a glance to determine. One usually decided the question in this manner: —

"But, if the nose also is false, it must be that the ancestor has been omitted from the picture. Assuredly a serious oversight on the part of the painter."

Young Jocelin, however, was a living voucher for the reputation of that painter. Only the year before, he had stood beneath the portrait, and, laying two fingers on the side of his nose, had said reflectively: —

"Even now it is almost as large as your own, mon aïeul."

It will be observed that Jocelin was French. The first part of the above remark is a translation, Jocelin's knowledge of English being limited, at that time, to such phrases as: "Ow do you do?" and "Mair Kreesmus!"

The French also was inherited from the ancestor. There were many things in the life of Jocelin, besides the nose, for which the ancestor was responsible. There was the artistic temperament, for example. The ancestor had written poems, and fairy tales, and masques. Other things also he had done which were not as beneficial to the race, but which were included in the inheritance. Jocelin had aristocratic blood in his veins, his mother said. It might easily be imagined.

There had been a title, too, but evidently it had not possessed the enduring qualities of the remainder of the endowment, for when Jocelin came into the world he came without it.

The ancestor had written poems and fairy tales; this Jocelin could never do. The music in him came, not from his brain, but from his lungs and vocal chords; and every low, sweet note of that strange child-voice was a revealing of the record of those lives, wild, passionate, dissolute, artistically tempered, from which Jocelin's frail, worn-out, young vitality had feebly taken its rise. But although the ancestor had, undoubtedly, much to answer for in regard to the constitutional weaknesses of his young kinsman, justice requires the statement that the boy's mother herself — she was not a descendant, being a kindly woman, but of no blood — was, to a large extent, accountable for the aggravation of those weaknesses. If she had had a grudge against him, some excuse could be made for her; but as she adored him, the fact that she reared him in his earliest infancy upon tea and claret is not easily pardoned.

At the age of two, Jocelin began to go to the opera, and long before he was out of dresses he was a connoisseur in voices and could tell you how different notes ought to be taken, and why such and such a singer failed to create an effect in such and such a melody. To hear his "Encore! encore! bravo!" when the tenor rendered

a difficult passage with especially careful art, or
to see him wince when the falcon's high notes
grew a shade too sharp, was as instructive and
entertaining as the opera itself. In the first
years of his attendance he sometimes dozed during the intermissions, if the previous act had not
been too exciting; but at the first of the three
raps which announced the rising of the curtain
he was awake, alert, on his feet, his chin resting
upon the velvet rim of the partition which separated the box from the aisle. It was always a
loge grillée, — a retired family box, excellent for
hearing, and for seeing, too, when the lattice was
thrown back, — the same box, year after year,
till it grew as homelike and familiar to him as
the picture of his ancestor.

This was before his father's death three years
ago. Since then, Jocelin had gone but seldom to
the opera, and when he did go he sat beside his
mother in the parquet and dangled his legs. It
was less comfortable, but it made him feel more
grown-up, and between the acts he was allowed
to go up in the foyer and the corridors. The
first time he did this, he peeped into "our box."
It was very rude of him, and, being a little
French boy, he realized it and said, "Pardon,
madame!" in his best manner to the lady who
sat there, but he could not help feeling as if she
and not he were the intruder.

This was only one of the changes apparently

due to the death of his father. Another, a less
important one in the eyes of Jocelin, was the
coming of Jeanne. She arrived about three
months after his father's departure, and he was
told that she was his sister. He took the announcement calmly, until some one said that her
appearance on the scene had put his nose out of
joint, and then he grasped his ancestral feature
and burst into tears, crying: —

"It is already so large that the boys laugh,
but to be out of joint as well, — oh, what an
affliction! "

But it came about gradually that, beyond the
fact that he found Jeanne a pretty plaything so
long as she did not pull his hair, — or his nose,
— she made very little difference in his comfort
or discomfort in this world. He had a way of
arranging his affairs to suit himself. His own
voice consoled him for the loss of the opera, and
of late he had discovered that Jeanne, too, could
sing, and he found it entertaining to teach her.

"O ma fille chérie, O ma fille chérie! "

There was a splashing to the right of the bath-
house, and presently another boy came walking
through the water and stood beside the ladder in
silence, save for his quick breathing. Jocelin
made no sign of recognition, but, directing his
eyes absently towards the new-comer, continued
to sing without a pause.

The water was very low under the bath-house; it came just above the boy's knees as he stood there, a sun-browned, glistening, sturdy thing, his legs planted apart, his hands on his hips, his muscular chest heaving. The water trickled down his chin, which was square and firm, and off the end of his straight nose; drops clung to the long dark lashes which shadowed his keen gray eyes. He tossed his close-cropped head and drew one arm smearingly across his face. He was attentive to the music; one could see that he enjoyed it healthily. He stared at Jocelin with flattering admiration; then (so quickly the thought came that his countenance did not change) he put forth his hand and tickled the sole of Jocelin's bare foot.

The melody ended with a howl and a French execration. The boy laughed, and Jocelin, raging and writhing, at last freed his insulted limb from the entangling ladder and kicked impatiently into the air.

"I swam from the big wharf," said the boy, also in French, standing at a safe but tantalizing distance and endeavoring to change the subject.

"Yanhh!" said Jocelin.

"I could hear you singing as far as that," the boy continued, with a placatory uplifting of his straight black brows.

"Then why didn't you stay there?" growled Jocelin, sullen but mollified.

"But you are conceited, yes!" The boy's eyebrows went up this time superciliously. "And you think I came all this way to hear you sing?"

"I despise you!" said Jocelin.

"I have some news."

"Keep it!"

"It concerns you!"

"You are a large bag of wind!"

"I intend to tell you, even if you do not wish to hear it."

"I shall stop my ears!" Jocelin attempted to suit the action to the word, but the ladder pinioned his arms. At best he could close but one ear, for if he freed both arms he must fall. He yelled to drown the offending communication, but the other boy shouted also. They were dreadful words; each one sounded as loud as the beat of a bass-drum in Jocelin's ears: —

"My father is going to marry your mother."

"You lie!" shrieked Jocelin.

"I shall punch your head!" said the boy, getting red and sending sparks from his gray eyes. "And I would assuredly do it, if you were not so little and scrawny, and younger than I."

"Who told you that?" demanded Jocelin.

"My father, and he does not tell a lie, — no, never! He said, 'My son, I have something of interest to communicate to you,' and he laid his hand upon my head." The boy laid his own hand upon an imaginary head descriptively.

"Then he said, ' Madame Castaigne has done me
the honor of accepting my addresses; the wedding
will take place in October, after we return to the
city. You will be a good son to her, my child!'
And I replied, ' Yes, my father,' and moreover
I did not cry like a baby." Large tears were
streaming down Jocelin's thin cheeks. "I went
down to the big wharf and I threw off my clothes
and dived over, and I heard you singing; so I
said to Antoine, who was fishing, ' You bring
my clothes to the Castaigne bath-house in your
pirogue; I shall dress there,' and I came to tell
you."

The boy used his hands while he spoke, and
his gestures gave color to his words, — one saw
him dive, and wave his farewell to the obliging
Antoine.

"I hear the boat now," he continued, and ran
out from under the bath-house, returning presently with a small bundle of blue cottonade and
white linen. It was apparent that his clothes
consisted of but two garments; nor could Jocelin
boast of more, — blue cottonade short trousers
and a white shirt with pink speckles in it, un-
buttoned at his brown bird-throat.

"I cannot see why my mother should desire to
marry your father," said Jocelin piteously, his
face streaked and wet with tears.

"As for my father, he is a very fine man,"
said the other vigorously. "I will not deny that

my taste is not his in the matter of wives. For myself, I prefer a woman who has not quite so markedly the figure of a cotton-bale; but my father is a man of individuality,— he does not go by the outside."

Jocelin's mouth, which had opened aggressively at the word "cotton-bale," closed with a baffled expression, and his future relative continued: —

"There will happily now be some one to touch you up on occasion with a peach-tree switch."

"And if he do I will kill him!" snarled Jocelin.

"Snipe!" said the other boy scornfully.

Jocelin was weeping from helpless rage. "And if I did not know that I must go to bed if I fall in the lake and these trousers are wet, I should come down and tear your face ; but it is not for your sake that I shall go to bed,— no!" he shouted vehemently.

There was a pitter-patter of little feet above on the wharf, and a baby voice called caressingly: —

"Jacques! Jacques!"

Jocelin still glowered, but the boy with the gray eyes elevated his chin and smiled.

"What then, my little one?" he called.

"I have come down the wharf, — alone, — me! — all the way!" chirped the voice.

A look of alarm came over the face of Jacques.

"And mammie, where, then, is she?"

"She sleeps! her mouth is open wide, like this!" A gesture evidently accompanied these words. "It was too tiresome for Jeanne, — Jeanne is here."

"Jeanne is naughty!" said the boy. "If she had fallen over the edge of the wharf! She must stay still till Jacques comes."

"Jeanne is not naughty!" said the voice emphatically. "Does she not lie even now on her stomach in the middle of the wharf, and the edges are far away?"

"I shall tell maman, and she will spank you!" said Jocelin sententiously.

"No, you will not tell maman, and she will not spank her!" This time Jacques' eyebrows were admonitory; then he smiled pleasantly and advanced towards Jocelin. "And meanwhile, Jojo, mon frère, as it is necessary that I should mount and put on my clothes, I shall be obliged to climb over you."

He grasped the sides of the ladder, and, putting his foot on the first step, raised himself face to face with the singer and paused ; something in Jocelin's acquiescent expression made him add before he climbed farther: "And if you bite me I shall assuredly kick some of your teeth down your throat!"

"I do not wish to have your distasteful flesh in my mouth!" sneered Jocelin, perjuring himself, but obtaining the last word. And the ascent was accomplished without accident.

In two minutes the bath-house door slammed and Jacques came out on the wharf. Jeanne was lying there patiently, poking her fingers into the cracks between the planks. He stooped down and lifted her up into his arms easily, for he was twelve years old and strong for his age.

"Look, then, at thy Jacques, thou mischief!" he said, and she looked, and put her arms around his neck and kissed him lightly on the nose.

The yellowest yellow hair had Jeanne, and the brownest brown eyes; there was a dimple in her chin, and her nose was tip-tilted. The paternal feature had been entirely expended upon Jocelin, and there was no choice left for Jeanne; she was obliged to derive her nose from her mother's side of the house, — such a pretty nose! Her cheeks were pink and plump, not brown and lean like Jocelin's. A very puff-ball of a baby, light as a fluff of down.

"And if Jeanne had fallen down, alone on the wharf, and no Jacques near to kiss the bobo?" said the boy.

"There are more times than one that Jacques is not near to kiss the bobo," returned Jeanne meditatively.

Jacques rubbed his hard young cheek against her downy pink one and laughed, and walked down the wharf carrying her.

"But Jacques will be always near hereafter," he said presently, struck with a sudden thought: "Jacques is to be thy brother, mignonne; tell him if thou art not glad?"

"But no!" said the baby, "Jocelin is my brother. Not more brother!"

"And Jacques also!" returned the boy. "Why not Jacques, bébé?"

Her lips quivered, and she flung out one little arm passionately. "Jacques said, 'Jacques is little husband, Jeanne is little wife.' Jocelin is my brother; is not one enough? Jacques is not my brother! Jacques is Jacques! Not brother! Not a brother! Brother naughty, — not Jacques naughty!"

He laughed at her distress and attempted to explain. "It is a thing that is unavoidable, my little one. Listen! It is not I who do this, it is my father. If he will marry thy mother, what can I do? — the thing is established by law. But what do I say to thee? Thou canst not comprehend, — eh, little sister?"

She was in truth sadly bewildered; her brow was puckered, and the tears were gathering in her brown, brown eyes. "Little sister and little wife also?" she said imploringly as the tear-drops fell.

Jacques' own idea of the limits and possibilities of this new relationship was hazy, and his propensity to tease was strong.

"I fear it would not be considered comme il faut," he replied with exaggerated gravity. "It might be possible if you had a dispensation from the Pope, but — well — you know the Pope! Such things are not obtained every day. For me, I am not hopeful."

This harangue was all Greek to the baby, but she understood that her desire was refused, and she opened her mouth and howled.

Jacques trudged along steadily, and allowed her to howl.

"But if it can't be helped, why should you cry?" he said presently in an argumentative tone which was entirely thrown away upon his little comrade, who had lost sight of her grief through her tears and was crying from pure momentum.

They had reached the end of the wharf. Farther down on the beach lay mammie asleep with her head propped on a log. The little wind that comes before a storm had arrived suddenly, and was blowing Jeanne's yellow curls; it brought with it Jocelin's voice from the bath-house, where he was singing again. A look of amazement came over the face of Jacques as he listened.

"Thy brother is a crocodile!" he said to Jeanne; "he sheds tears for grief, but he was not sorrowful — no! — hear him sing! He does not care. He has no bowels within him; he is nothing but voice." He threw his head back, and his chin was very square. He spoke to himself this time: —

"I did not shed one tear yet, — no! Oh, my father! you and I, — we were sufficient; why not? That Jocelin! That snipe! I would wish to punch his head! But if he had my lump in his throat he could not sing, — no!"

The baby's wail, which had died to a whimper, was beginning to reassume its crescendo-forte proportions, but Jacques turned and cried: —

"Tr-r-r-oum, boum, boum, it is fate!" in a tremendous voice, with a terrifying Mephistophelian depression of his expressive brows, like the man in the play, and she stopped, reduced to silence through intellectual bewilderment. She continued to stare at him in a dazed, baby fashion as they walked, and he laughed at her blank little countenance; and then the raindrops began to come down, and he ran to the house.

Jocelin, who would have been quite safe if he had remained under the bath-house, came home instead and was very wet, and was put to bed, because that was the third pair of cottonade trousers he had spoiled that day.

"Jocelin is thy little brother; I am thy big brother," said Jacques, as he sat on the gallery floor amusing the baby; but she shook her head solemnly and said, "Jacques not say that! makes Jeanne a bobo in her stomach."

And when the wedding day came, no one could understand why the little Jeanne, who was usually so well-behaved and self-possessed, cried very loud in the middle of the ceremony for two minutes. Nobody knew but Jacques, who was supporting her on the back of the pew, and said softly, inspired by a spirit of mischief: —

"Now thou art little sister! It is accomplished!"

And Jocelin sang a solo in the organ loft like an angel.

BOOK I

SPINSTERS ALL AND BACHELORS MERRY

> " What shall arrive with the cycle's change ?
> A novel grace and a beauty strange.
> I will make an Eve, be the artist that began her,
> Shaped her to his mind ! "
>
> ROBERT BROWNING.

CHAPTER I

A FAMILY COUNCIL

MONSIEUR DUMARAIS sat in his armchair by the window, his hands clasped tensely before him, his sensitive, clear-cut face gray with suppressed emotion, and rigidly blank. He had not, as yet, spoken in the discussion; he had kept the words back between his thin lips and his clenched teeth, — they were hard words of rebellion.

There was just now a lull in the conversation. Jacques had pushed his chair away from the breakfast-table and sunk himself into it, his hands in his trousers' pockets, his head thrust down between his shoulders. He was thinking the matter over intently. Jocelin, long, thin, and languid, flicked bread-crumbs across the table-cloth with sullen indifference. He had the air of one who knows himself a culprit, this Jocelin, but persists in demanding sympathy. Madame Dumarais held the letter in her fat hands close to her fat chins and read it over her spectacles. Behind her stood Jeanne, impatiently twisting from one foot to the other.

All these things Monsieur Dumarais could not see, but he could feel them, — he was blind.

Jacques slid up into the seat of his chair and turned to his father.

"Eh bien, mon père, what is it that you have to advise in the matter? We have not heard your voice as yet."

Then Monsieur Dumarais spoke, and his words were a torrent.

"What should I say? What should I advise? Am I anything, that I should speak? To sit here day after day eating the bread of idleness is not bitterness enough, but I must also be mocked with authority! My son asks permission to put bread into my mouth. This is what it is to be a man! Were I a woman, I should knit; I might at least be able to deceive myself into thinking that I was not wholly useless and dependent. To sit in the dark and listen to the makeshifts which are devised to keep the wolf from the door! To remember that when these eyes could guide these hands, there was no advice in this house, — there was my will! There was then no one who insulted us for charity's sake!"

He paused, shaking in his chair, with beads of perspiration standing out on his ghastly forehead. Madame cast up her eyes, her hands, her shoulders, silently, in resigned, apologetic pity. Jeanne's eyes widened with fright, and sought Jacques' steady, clean-shaven face with the square, determined chin.

"It is not an insult, my father," said Jacques;

"it is simply this friend of Jeanne who visited the Chesters last winter and spent an evening here, you will remember. She had a voice like a poll-parrot, but that is not visible in her letter. Of course it is quite clear that she wants her friends to stay here, but that appeals to me in the light of a compliment rather than an insult, — you will appreciate my unbounded conceit, my father!"

Jacques smiled jocosely, and the situation seemed to grow less tense.

"And, moreover, she is most delicate in her manner of not saying so. These things are done every day now. I can see that it will be a relief to her if we take them. She asks if we can suggest any French family who would be willing to receive them; and she adds that she would be glad to feel they were coming to us, but she feels that is not to be thought of. It is a most courteous letter. She was not to me an interesting woman, and no doubt her friends are stiff, Northern old maids with cranks; but it is a most courteous letter, notwithstanding. You know, my father, that we have not yet come to want, and it is my joy and privilege to provide for you and maman and Jeanne; but I thought, as so much expense had been incurred unavoidably of late," — Jocelin's hand shook as he flicked his crumbs, — "that it would make maman happier if she had this money all her own in addition. But if you

prefer that it should not be so, we will not speak
of it again."

"It is now two years that the Bonets have had
a boarder, and Monsieur Bonet in good health
and having also a fine situation in that rice-mill.
No one considers such things these days," observed Madame Dumarais in a tone of self-justi-
fication. "And the Martineaus, three boarders
this year, one of them a child, — but I would not
take a child, no! And those girls go everywhere,
and who remarks? And the Barbiers! Who is
it that stands better in the city than the Barbiers?
He was a friend of your papa, Jocelin, Monsieur
Barbier. It was only last week Madame Barbier said to me, 'We like it, these quiet times; it
makes the house a little gay.'"

Madame Dumarais was beginning to feel that
every respectable family ought to possess at least
one boarder.

"I do not anticipate that they will be gay,
these women," said Jacques sarcastically.
"Noisy, doubtless, with that disagreeable, hard
voice of the North. But as for gayety! these
Northerners do not understand how to enjoy themselves; that is an established fact. Ours will be
old maids, mournful and cranky, drinking a
great deal of tea, and shocked at the sight of the
claret on the table."

"Grand Dieu, seigneur!" exclaimed Jocelin,
"and are we then to keep the claret off the table?"

Madame Dumarais and Jeanne looked helplessly at Jacques, who replied emphatically: —

"Je dis non! they have come to see a French
family. Let them see, let them learn! We live
as we have always lived."

Madame turned the letter irresolutely in her
pudgy fingers and glanced at her husband, who
was calm now, but looked discouraged and weary.

"Only for a little frolic we will take them this
winter," faltered madame. "It will not be for
always; we have enough without. But it will be
cheerful for Jacques and Jocelin with two young
ladies in the house. It will be an education for
Jeanne; her English is not what it should be."

Jacques laughed, and madame blushed and
smiled apologetically.

"Then it is decided!" cried Jeanne with a
little skip, and Jacques arose and went over to
his father's chair.

"You will allow maman the pleasure of this
little frolic, mon père," he said caressingly; "you
will allow Jeanne to do this kindness for her
friend who has written the charming letter?
These people who are coming are desirous of
dwelling in a family, not a boarding-house. You
will allow us to gratify them? If Jeanne and
maman were to go away for their health, would
not you be the first to demand that they should
live with people who could be their friends and
could chaperon them?"

Monsieur Dumarais lifted his face towards the voice of Jacques: —

"I am a proud old man, my son," he said; "proud, and sensitive, and unreasonable. Mon Dieu! what can you expect at my age? Do as you think best. Far be it from me to refuse to shelter two harmless women. It will also be a relief to your mother at times to have money of her own to spend on little extravagancies for which she need be accountable to no one."

And from this it might be inferred that Monsieur Dumarais, although blind, had as keen an insight into the situation as any one present. Madame and Jocelin grew red, and avoided each other's eyes.

"Go, Jeanne, and write the letter," said Jacques, smiling. "Tell thy friend the poll-parrot that her old maids may come here, and we shall do our best to make the winter agreeable. Go, then! I will take it with me to the post."

"Me!" exclaimed Jeanne with a gasp of terror; "but I can never do that! A letter in English! Oh, Jacques! Why not maman? Or thou, Jacques, thou? Thou art so fluent with the English, writing letters all day long."

"Ah, bah!" said Jacques. "And is it to me, this letter, this request? And thou, having been for two years at an English school, — thou canst not write a letter?"

"But, Jacques, yes! a school letter. Never

to a real person, and this thought makes me afraid."

Jeanne's face was a picture of childish distress; she was most unhappy. So Jacques made a great noise in pulling forward a little table and storming about for ink and a pen. And where was Jeanne's best paper, with her monogram upon it, which he gave her on her last birthday? For what was it intended if not for such a moment as this? And finally he had seated Jeanne at the little table, and she was writing, at his dictation, while her heart fluttered, a letter which appeared to her to be a miracle of English. For he was a man of affairs, this marvelous Jacques, and one must speak much that is not French if one would be successful on the Cotton Exchange, even in New Orleans. And Jacques was successful.

"Was there any arrangement about the amount of board?" asked Jocelin in a low tone, pausing beside his mother as he sauntered out of the room.

"Not yet," she answered, and glanced apprehensively at the blind man by the window.

CHAPTER II

JACQUES' OWN WAY

JACQUES had always been able to do the thing he wished to do, and he was now twenty-eight years old. One's habits are beginning to toughen and take root at that age. Moreover, it is a long time to be allowed to have one's own way,—twenty-eight years.

If you had intimated to Jacques that he always did as he pleased, he would have laughed good-naturedly, and told you that you were confusing him with Jocelin. But it was not true that Jocelin always had his own way, and no one knew this better than Jocelin himself. It was because the desires that he was able to satisfy were so often satisfied at the expense of the feelings of other people that he had acquired a reputation for self-indulgence, but there were other desires which remained unsatisfied — at the expense of his own feelings.

Jacques' world was all one color. Having always had his own way, he was entirely uncon-scious of the fact. There had been no change in his life to thrust it upon him, and the only other

way of becoming aware of it — that of observing
the play of such contrast in the lives of others
— was not his way; his own affairs kept him sufficiently occupied. Whether or not he possessed
the grace of sacrificing his desires to those of
other people is at present beside the question; no
such sacrifice had hitherto been required of him,
because all that he had ever wished to do had
been so entirely the outcome of rigid common
sense, so unquestionably healthful and beneficial
for those over whom he had exercised authority,
that, even if they wanted to do otherwise, they
were ashamed to say so. And almost always
when, as sometimes happened with Jocelin, they
did otherwise without saying anything about it,
they came to grief.

To some people responsibility is as the breath
of life, and this was true of Jacques. There
were times when, on being joked by his friends
about his latest fancy, he would look grave almost
to sadness and reply: —

"Ah! but you know it would be impossible for
me, in my present position, to marry; I could
not afford the expense of another family."

And at such moments he thought it mattered
a great deal to him, — this virtuous abstention
from matrimony, — but it did n't.

Jacques had been at the head of his family
ever since he was sixteen, when his father began
to lose his eyesight; but he had controlled his

own affairs for a much longer period, and he had them under excellent control.

Monsieur Dumarais — before his blindness an excellent accountant on a large salary — had spent two thirds of his waking hours at his desk, and the remaining third in reading his Paris journals and keeping himself thoroughly in touch with the best French literature of the day; so that his young son, motherless from the age of three, had ample opportunity for developing the energetic obstinacy, and the talent for decisive, practical action, which were to distinguish him in later life.

He was a bookworm, Monsieur Dumarais. As he leaned against his office-desk, there was always a paper-covered book bulging out of his pocket. When he went to and from his day's work, he held the book in his hand with his forefinger between the leaves, and on certain quiet blocks he read as he walked. In summer he irresolutely stopped to rest in the large square near his house, and here some of the children usually lay in wait to decoy him home, — after the second Madame Dumarais, having endured the ruin of several good dinners, had been instructed in his habits by Jacques. He pursued a swift, never-ending journey from literature to ledgers and back again, and one day, somewhere midway in this race from desire to necessity, his weary eyes lagged behind his persistent spirit, — lagged farther and farther, day by day, — until finally they never caught up any more.

Monsieur Dumarais was very bitter.

"If I had known that this was to happen, I would never have married again," he said to Jacques. He said it again and again as the years passed; it seemed to be the only atonement he could make; but it embarrassed Jacques, who was wont to say, "Ah, bah!" gruffly, and change the subject.

Just what had been monsieur's motive in making this second marriage was never quite clearly defined. There were those on the lake shore, that summer when he made his declaration, who insisted that madame had set her cap for him most shamefully, — fat, sentimental madame. There were others, more charitable, who said that he had taken a wife for the sake of his little son; and these usually predicted trouble, affirming that the boy was an independent fellow, and had been left to his own devices too long to be made amenable to petticoat government at this late date.

But the predictions of trouble were not verified. The relations between Jacques and his step-mother were marked from the first by peace and good-nature. Madame Dumarais was not one to make trouble. Nothing could have induced her to interfere with the inclinations for good or evil of even the most helpless infant in arms, much less the determined will of a vigorous twelve-year-old boy like Jacques.   Madame's most positive emotion was timidity.   There was nothing in life of which she was not just a little afraid, — no situation before which she did not quail.   Little noises made her white or pink; little alarms deprived her of the power of speech. She was afflicted with a chronic faint-hearted-ness, and every flutter of her mind was made manifest to the public eye through the fatty vibrations of her body.   And yet a physician would have been reluctant to label this state as nerves, — madame's was a simple organism, akin to that of the jelly-fish.

When she married Monsieur Dumarais she kissed Jacques on both cheeks, — large, sprawly kisses with a great deal of loose sound about them, — and then she smiled a frightened, depre-catory smile down into his unsentimental gray eyes.   It was a part of the ceremony, and he expected it.   If his eyes were alert and keen, it was mere habit, and not because he was studying her.   He had finished studying her some time be-fore.   He knew she was frightened, and he had expected that, too.   He was very well acquainted with this step-mother.

"She will mend my clothes," he reasoned within himself, "and the clothes of my father and Jocelin and Jeanne.   That will be pleasant. But she will never say No.   Why?   She is afraid, but it is not all fear.   She is very soft."

Farther than this, Jacques' metaphysical specu-
lations did not lead him, but this was far enough
for all practical emergencies. So he continued
to make changes in his winter and summer under-
clothing at what seasons suited him best, after
his father's marriage, as he had done before. He
bathed as many times a day in summer, and
studied as many lessons in winter, as he chose,
and in both cases his choice was up to the maxi-
mum limit. He went to the American University rather than the Jesuits' College, because he
wished to, and, having started in the preparatory
department, his English became as accurate as
that of his school-fellows, which is not saying
much for it, after all. He studied from love of
conquest, from necessity of dominating whatever
he attacked, and because he was overflowing with
energy.

Energy is not usually considered a creole trait,
but Monsieur Dumarais, although a boy when he
came to America, was a Parisian of the Parisians;
and young Jacques, being, as it were, the first
stop-cock from the source of supply, set free a
flow of energetic power more than sufficient in
force and volume to run three step-families of
the size of the one already in its way. Fortunate Jacques! to be in at the beginning, where
one tingled with the rush and the shock of the
tearing stream. Farther away, in the days of
the third and fourth generations, perhaps the

stream might only percolate. Jocelin, for example, was a third or fourth generation. He felt no rush and tug of energy,— no! as the slow drops percolated they tickled him, and he liked being tickled; he only lay the stiller to catch the sensation. But Jacques never stayed still. He was a noisy boy. He had a big Ha-ha! — just two great laughs that clapped against each other and set in motion the smaller laughters of everybody else who chanced to be near. When he came in from school, he banged his books down, and shouted out the events of the day with a radiant enjoyment that was infectious; and when he left school and went to work, he continued to behave in the same effervescent manner, transforming the dinner-table into an impromptu cotton exchange by the very atmosphere which he brought to it.

The summer that he was sixteen he worked in a cotton-broker's office as under-clerk and errand-boy. Because he wanted to, of course.

"But to seek work when one has a vacation, and moreover when the weather is hot!" said Jocelin, eying him with a look of troubled aversion.

"Why not?" said Jacques. He had no capacity for lolling around the house, smoking cigarettes and strumming the piano; he was not languid, and too tall for his age, and too thin, like Jocelin. He was compactly built, quick in his

motions as in his speech, actively alive. He
enjoyed the Cotton Exchange with a healthy, unmoral ardor; it was a place of action, and action
was life to him.

And then, in the middle of the summer, his
father had a fright with his eyes, and there was
a lightning flash in Jacques' quick mind which
left him quivering with an excitement that was
half joy, half fear. He had a sudden luminous
foreboding of the responsibility to come, and it
made him keen to test his strength, and frightened with a terror that is courage. It was never
Jacques' way to discuss his motives, to enter
into long and satisfactory explanations for doing
things; and when he announced in the autumn
that he was not going back to the University, it
was an announcement pure and simple.

His step-mother cried, "But, Jacques!" and
looked helpless, and his father turned slowly
white and said, "Why is this, my son?" — said it
as if he were afraid of the answer. Monsieur
Dumarais had had another fright about his eyes.

The answer was not alarming. Jacques intended to be a business man, and he had gotten
a good foothold in his present position. The firm
liked him; he was popular with the men around
the Exchange; there was a chance of making his
way upward, and such chances were not found
every day. He could not see how two more
years at the University would help him to be a

better cotton man. In short, he wanted to do it.
Why not? And Monsieur Dumarais, with that
sick fear cold within him, dared not bring forth
his valid, intellectual arguments against the
brisk "Why not?" lest he should discover that
Jacques had other reasons at his command.

• That was twelve years ago, and to-day Jacques
was a man on 'Change, with an interest in the
profits of the firm. He was the clever man of
the firm, and they did not want to do without
him; so they gave him an interest to keep him
quiet. He was worth more than they gave, and
he knew it; but being unable, through lack of
money, to go into business for himself, he was,
as he darkly expressed it to Jeanne, lying in wait
for a capitalist. And little Jeanne laughed with
delight, partly because she thought, from Jacques'
eyes, that it was a joke, and any joke of his must
of course be more. enjoyable than the jokes of
other people; but chiefly she laughed because his
mocking eyes were looking into her own, and the
words were said to her in a whisper of ironic confidence; to her, — to her! Reason enough, surely,
for the joy in her heart that sent that pretty
laugh to her lips! But nobody knew less about
her heart and its whys and wherefores than
Jeanne.

Jacques' other relatives were more or less passive in their submission to his will, but Jeanne
demanded to be ruled. It was an active pleasure

to her to obey Jacques, and, even though she did
his behests with tears in her eyes, there was
contentment in her soul. To do the thing that
Jacques wished her to do! truly what higher aim
could one desire in life? When he spoke to her
the brown eyes, turned wide to him, seemed seeking — what? Jeanne? But she did not know how
to ask herself questions. And Jacques? — did
he ask himself any?

Jacques' will, to those who loved it, was, on
the whole, a pleasant one. It took Jeanne away
from the French Roman Catholic school when she
was fifteen, and sent her up town across Canal
Street to an English private school, where, if she
did not learn much from her books, her shy,
pretty manners gained a certain polish which
made their very shyness more fascinating, and
contact with American girls gave her confidence,
if not accuracy, in speaking English. Jacques'
will also kept her from making her début into
society as early as Madame Dumarais had taken
it for granted that she should.

"He has some curious ideas, your brother.
He becomes more and more American." And
madame was not quite clear in her mind as to
whether she meant to express disapproval or the
contrary by this remark. It never occurred to
her, however, to rebel against the "curious ideas,"
although — and this may seem paradoxical —
madame was less afraid of this noisy, efficient

step-son than of any other member of her family.

Jeanne did not care about the début, at least not much. The clothes of course would be entertaining, but Jacques thought nineteen was young enough for a débutante, and naturally, if Jacques thought so, you know! — This was a year ago. Jeanne was nineteen now and winter had arrived, and doubtless she would be allowed to go to all the balls; for the two old maids were coming, and Jacques had said in the letter that they were to have a pleasant time. Jeanne had never been to a ball; that was another of Jacques' ideas: he said balls were not a place for children, even if the children wore high-necked white muslins and sat all the evening in a *loge grillée*. But occasionally she had misgivings about these Northern women.

"Dost thou think, Jacques, that, being old maids, they will have a desire to go to balls?" she questioned doubtfully.

"They will adore balls," Jacques assured her; "thou dost not know the human nature of an old maid, my child."

This he said looking up at her as he went downstairs the night of the arrival of the guests. He was going to meet them.

"Au revoir, bébé!" he called, as he walked along the brick passageway to the door. He was thinking: "There will not be any prettier at the balls this year. She is indeed beautiful at times."

And he mentally reviewed her eyes, her nose, her mouth, the color of her hair and the way it grew upon her forehead, dwelling upon each feature, each attribute, in turn, with critical satisfaction. At Canal Street he quickened his pace to a brisk, swinging walk, and his mind turned to more important matters.

"I shall do this, — I shall do that, — I shall do the other."

This was the tenor of his thoughts as he made his way down towards the river-end of the broad, gay street. Plans, combinations, decisions! — Jacques had many on hand, all prospering.

"These are the things that I shall do."

Shall do! Shall do! There was no "if" among his words.

Ah, the complacent fatness of a contented mind!

CHAPTER III

THE ARRIVAL

JACQUES was thinking intently, while he paced the ill-lighted platform before the waiting-room with unconcerned audibleness. He set his chin more firmly and drew his eyebrows close together.

The night was clear and mild, as nights so often are in New Orleans in December, and presently the train, which was late, would roll in, past the platform, under the open sky. On other nights, when it rained and the train rolled in just the same, Northern visitors felt that it was a very open sky indeed; and as they groped around sloppily between the tracks, they said unfriendly things about the Southern hospitality that dumped its guests out in the mud at such a time, and let them scurry for shelter as best they might. But in fine weather — the soft, traditional weather of the South — strangers noted only the blue darkness and the stars. This is what they would do to-night.

Jacques paused beside a lamp and looked at his watch; but this attention to external affairs was purely involuntary, for it was not the coming

of the maiden ladies which caused that thoughtful
wrinkle between his brows.

Some three weeks before, there had come to
the city with a party of railroad magnates a
young New Yorker, a man of thirty or there-
abouts, dilettante, idle, and overburdened with
riches. Through somebody on the Cotton Exchange to whom he had letters, he met Jacques,
and took a fancy to him, following him about in
the uneasy fashion common to unoccupied men,
taking him off to luncheon, and inventing excuses
for delaying him on street corners. When the
railroad men went off in their private car, and
Jacques found Curtis Baird still loitering about
the Cotton Exchange, he felt for this wretchedly
wealthy young cynic and philosopher something
that was at once envy and pity and contempt.
But when Baird had for three days ingeniously
turned every subject of conversation into a discussion of Jacques' ability and Jacques' prospects, and accompanied this discussion by an
undercurrent of comment upon his own devil-
may - care attitude and lack of occupation,
Jacques' mind emitted a second prophetic flash,
similar to the one which had inspired him years
before, and aghast, he said within himself: —

"Behold! The capitalist!"

Then that involuntary muscle of the mind which
is the instinct of an honorable man reacted with
a jerk, and drew Jacques up sharp on the defen-
sive.

"If this misanthrope has anything to say to me, he may say it, but if he thinks I 'm the kind of deadbeat that will assist him to say it " —

Here Jacques' thoughts seethed into an emotional desire to kick the man who should so dare to impugn his honor.

But after another week Mr. Baird, having felt his way with all the ironic distrust and self-contemptuous alertness of the skeptic, came to the point and made his proposition like a gentleman. Small wonder was it that Jacques had little space in his soul for the contemplation of imaginary old maids. He had had the thing on his mind for two days now, and he had kept it close, even from his father. He had not given his answer, and was not to give it for a month, unless he chose; but as he walked the platform this evening he was trailing air-castles at every step, — business air-castles, of course, crammed full of cotton-futures.

And then the train rolled in, and he went down across the tracks, his thoughts one blur for the moment, as happens sometimes when one is compelled to make a sudden readjustment of time and place in dropping from dreams to reality. Before this readjustment had taken place, Jacques' automatic centres — it must have been his automatic centres, for there was no other reason for his remarkable course of action — had carried him across the track and brought him

to a standstill before — two women? Yes, of
course! but why these two? He raised his hat
to one of them with the same precision which had
characterized his previous actions, and said: —

"Miss Spenser, I believe?" And then, having
arrived at full consciousness, he was about to
add, "Pray pardon me, I have made a mistake!"
when he realized that the lady was saying: —

"This is Mr. Dumarais, is it not? Miss Bennett and I had decided that it must be, when we
saw you leave the platform."

For a moment Jacques was stunned. When
he had assumed the responsibility of the bags,
and was piloting his companions along Canal
Street in search of the proper down-town car, he
was obliged to fight down a strong inclination to
stand still in the middle of the street and laugh ;
but he succeeded in finding the car without making himself conspicuous, and as they jingled down
one of the narrow French thoroughfares he was
able to collect himself, and recover to some extent
from his astonishment.

"A mule-car, Sylvia!" said Miss Spenser.
"The last time we rode in a mule-car we were in
Naples."

She said it with a reminiscent glow in her
voice, and Sylvia, without turning, smiled at her
out of the darkness in a sad, preoccupied fashion.
There was not any blue nor brown in Sylvia's
eyes; they were gray, the color of smoke, almost

black, soft and dusky behind the shadows of the long dark lashes. Jacques had gray eyes, too, but there was a steel sword-flash in them and a sparkle that was blue. Sylvia's eyes never flashed, but the fire of her soul burned, intense and steady, behind the smoke and through the soft darkness. She had a very still face. Some faces are blank from lack of power to receive impressions; but we do not call them still, although they are immovable. Sylvia's face was quiet with the rapt stillness of constant receptivity. She was pale, too, to-night, from the journey, and her friend involuntarily moved nearer to her and drew the wrap more closely about her throat.

Jacques made the usual commonplace remarks about journeys and fatigue and the weather, until it was time to jerk the bell-strap and stop the car; and in another minute the three were standing on a narrow, unevenly paved sidewalk in a narrow, dark street, down the centre of which the mule-car leisurely jingled. The houses, huddled close together, some high and some low, made a broken line against the sky down both sides of the street; and the balconies jutting out at irregular intervals, and from irregular heights, over the sidewalk projected quaint masses of black shadow into the already self-evident darkness.

Jacques stood in a grim, arched doorway, before a dingy, ancient double door, fitting a latch-key into an incongruous modern Yale lock.

From somewhere above, faint sounds of music came down to them, and as one half of the door swung back and let them into a wide brick passageway, these sounds became more distinct and resolved themselves finally into words: —

"Toujours," sang a man's voice wistfully, and again, "Toujours."

Some one played a pathetic strain on a piano, and the refrain came again, softly, slowly: —

> "Je rêve aux étés qui demeurent
> Toujours."

Then the piano dreamily.

Broad steps came down from the inside of the house to a door at one side of the passage. This door was not blank and sullen like the one which opened upon the street; it was light, with panes of glass half way down, and had white curtains behind it, looped back to show the wide, shallow stairs. At the other end of the passage there was an open arch, from which hung a severe iron lamp, and beyond, leaves flickered in the dim lamplight.

While the piano played, the two women tiptoed down to the arch and Jacques followed them. Standing beneath the lamp, they looked into a courtyard, bricked like the passage, and containing several square parterres raised about a foot from the pavement and neatly inclosed by the bricks. A large water-jar stood in one corner of the court, and the latticed galleries of the house inclosed the court on two sides, while the blank walls of other houses, of different heights, shut in the two remaining sides. The light from an open window above the arch was reflected upon the blank wall opposite, and through this window the music came quite clearly now, and the singer was beginning again: —

> " Ici-bas les lèvres effleurent
> Sans rien laisser de leur velours;
> Je rêve aux baisers qui demeurent
> Toujours."

"Sully Prudhomme!" whispered Enid Spenser excitedly, touching Sylvia.

"He is a favorite with my father," explained Jacques, also in a whisper.

"Toujours," sang the voice, thrilling with passionate anticipation.

"But — the — music?" murmured Enid, looking afar off as she tried to recall the melody.

"My little sister has composed the music," said Jacques simply. "It is she also who plays. The voice is my brother's."

> " Je rêve aux baisers qui demeurent
> Toujours."

Then, as they listened once more to the accompaniment, Jacques gave them the piece of information which he had been desirous of imparting all along.

"My father is blind," he said; "will you pardon me if I ask you now to go up to him, and speak to him each one in turn as I give him your names? He is able to distinguish by the voice."

"We shall be only too glad to do so," Enid answered, and Sylvia's eyes were wide with pity as her lips smiled assent.

They went to the glass doors after that and up the stairs, and the voice sang with a low wail of hunger and hopefulness: —

> "Ici-bas tous les hommes pleurent
> Leurs amitiés ou leurs amours;
> Je rêve aux couples qui demeurent
> Toujours."

Ah, the tears and the longing in the sweet voice!

> "Tou . . . jours."

They waited outside the parlor door for the refrain. Hope was strong in that last line: —

> "Je rêve aux couples qui demeurent
> Toujours."

The room which they entered was large, and full of clumsy dark furniture, whose ancient and harmonious dignity was impertinently modernized by fluffy, dangling, bright-colored tissue-paper balls and flowers, and cheap, home-made tidies. Two or three fine old-fashioned portraits shared the walls with plaques, celluloid Christmas cards, and a colored crayon drawing of a lady and an urn, done by madame in her youth. The carpet, once handsome enough of its kind, with a gigantic medallion pattern woven through it in decided

colors, was worn and mellowed now to a real
beauty; and a new and gaudy rug, in scarlet and
green, lay before the small open grate.

Jeanne turned on the piano stool and sat there,
round-eyed, staring at the new-comers with all her
astonished might as Jacques led them across the
room to his step-mother.

Madame blinked a little at Jacques, and regarded him for a moment with an absolutely
vacant countenance as he spoke to her; then, becoming aware of the two women beside him, she
staggered to her feet in a shaky, jellied fashion,
turned several shades of pink, and smiled uncertainly, her head on one side.

Jocelin had moved one, two, slow steps away
from the piano, looking at Sylvia. He seemed
unconscious of his movement, but he stopped and
watched her. It was as if he walked in his sleep
and stood still to see a dream pass by. Fortunately she was not looking at him; she had turned
away to where Monsieur Dumarais stood beside
his chair, waiting with the embarrassed uncertainty of the blind.

"Miss Spenser, may I present my father?"
said Jacques.

Enid's words came from her lips as if they
were the clear strokes of a bell. She had remembered that monsieur distinguished by the voice.

"We are so grateful to you for taking us into
your home," she began; "we are so happy to be

here. We thank you for giving us this pleasure, Mr. Dumarais."

"The pleasure is ours, mademoiselle," returned the old gentleman with an impressive bow.

"Miss Bennett, my father," Jacques continued.

Sylvia came a step nearer to the blind man and hesitated. The room was very quiet for a moment, but at last she said: —

"I also care for Sully Prudhomme, Mr. Dumarais. Will you let me talk with you about him some day? I have with me a little new edition of his poems which it might interest you to — to — hear about."

She had meant to say "see," but she had remembered. Jacques realized, with a start, that he had not heard her voice before, — a voice like a long sigh. Jocelin was motionless as one rapt in prayer.

Monsieur put out his hand with an eager, trembling gesture, and Sylvia laid her own in it and looked at him so that it seemed as if she must compel his sight.

"It will indeed be a happiness to me, mademoiselle," he said, with great simplicity and sweetness.

By this time Jeanne had sidled up to Jacques and was ready with her shy greeting, remnants of childlike astonishment still lingering in her wide-open eyes. And then it was Jocelin's turn, but Jocelin only bowed very low.

A period of stiffness followed, during which
Enid and Sylvia sat on one of the rosewood and
faded damask sofas and chatted politely, until
madame, having interpreted the enigmatic hints
conveyed by Jacques' gesticulatory eyebrows,
arose with a jump and stammered: —

"You — you — m-must have much fatigue; I
weel assist you to your rooms."

Jeanne assisted them also, and Jocelin went
down into the courtyard and paced the alleys
between the parterres with a cigarette.

In his dusky corner Monsieur Dumarais sat
with a delightful smile of quizzical amusement
upon his lips, and when he heard his son ap-
proaching the smile grew veritably mischievous;
but he said nothing, and Jacques, standing before
him, caught the look and burst out with his big
laugh. He and his father were the only ones
who saw the joke.

CHAPTER IV

TWO OLD MAIDS

ENID always had to spend a long time arranging her hair at night; it was such heavy hair, like a mane, burnished bronze, with a big ripple along its length now and then. Enid was tall and broad and strong; her skin was smooth; her flesh was firm; her eyes were brown and clear, with golden lights in them, like the lights in her hair.

She stood before the mirror to-night, her wrapper falling straight down around her, one arm, half bare, holding a mass of clinging hair above her head. She was a beautiful woman. People always knew at once that she was somebody. It was not her physique that produced this impression; she might have been statuesque and still have remained merely one among many handsome parlor ornaments. It was the large, observant, judicial gaze which distinguished her, the look as of one having authority. Her motions, too, expressed that dignified preoccupation, that complete emancipation from self-consciousness, which is sometimes the mark of one who has taken a stand in the world and has been recognized.

Enid had touched success, and the manifestation of the glory had not departed from her; she was as yet clothed in an atmosphere that was radiant. It is a wonderful thing to touch success when one is young,— a wonderful thing, but perilous, there is so much of life still to be lived afterwards. Enid was twenty-eight, and in these days success is very like a miracle at twenty-eight. It means that he who succeeds is unusually clever, or that, for the moment, the world is unusually appreciative. One trembles a little when the world has sudden fits of appreciativeness, — because it is such a cruel world.

But Enid did not tremble. She seldom indulged in uncomfortable forebodings; her mind was intensely but healthily occupied with a number of important matters, none of which pertained directly to herself. She had a long experience, through her friendship with Sylvia, of the kind of mind that discerns the moral, spiritual, and intellectual pitfalls which lie upon every pathway in life, and she had a tender and loving sympathy for all such minds, but she could not allow herself the time for speculation of that order. Time was very precious to Enid. Perhaps that was why she had accomplished so much in her short life. Perhaps that was why at twenty-eight she was already a figure of importance in her own community.

Enid had not written a book, — no. Nor yet
was she a poet. She was a teacher of History
and Social Science, she had several private
classes among women, and she gave lectures. It
was through the lectures that she had become
known. They were brilliant pieces of work, and
were received with the enthusiasm which was
their due. Her very youth helped her in gaining
her audiences. It made the reserved, old-fashioned people lenient towards her radicalism,
while at the same time it gave fresh impetus to
the hopes of the radicals. The best people knew
Enid's name now, and scholars, professors, and
specialists received her with respect as an equal.
Deep down within herself Enid took their homage
with the humility and prayerful reverence, and
also with the skeptical perception of its value as
a vanity of vanities, which are the bulwarks of
a large soul; but it helped her, nevertheless, more
than she realized, in the doing of her work.

Her face was vividly awake as she arranged
her hair, and now and then her lips moved unconsciously. Finally she flung back the two long
heavy tails which she had been braiding, and
stood still as if listening, but everything was
quiet; so she lowered the gas and moved across
the large, square room to Sylvia's door.

Sylvia was sitting half dressed and very quiet
in an armchair.

"Didn't I just know it?" said Enid, in tones

of accusation; "I said, ' She is sitting there not
moving a muscle, and she is tired all to little
bits.'" Then, with gentle playfulness, "I wish
you would get up and scream and throw things
and be violent, Sylvia, when you are tired; it
would be such a pleasure to me to have you do
that, instead of sitting so abnormally still."

She flung herself down by the armchair and
laid one arm across Sylvia's knee. Sylvia patted
the arm indulgently and said, after a moment, in
her low, musical monotone: —

"The face of the young man who sang haunts
me."

Enid gave a little gasp. "That I should live
to hear you say you were haunted by the face of
a man!" she gurgled indistinctly against her
friend's knee; and then, lifting her head, "True!
he did have the very largest nose I ever saw."

Sylvia leaned her head against the back of the
chair and laughed, a soft, sudden little laugh.

"I do not remember his nose," she said. "He
was looking straight at me, and he had the saddest eyes, as if the world were a hurt to him and
he asked the reason why."

"The world is a hurt to a good many of us,"
said Enid restlessly.

Sylvia looked distressed. "I don't believe he
meant the same kind of hurt," she said hesitatingly. "I — I — wasn't thinking of that kind
when I said it."

"No, dear, I know you were n't, I understood,"
returned Enid; "only it happened to make me
think of that kind of hurt. I did n't mean to
pervert your words."

There was a short silence, and then she said
suggestively, "Bed, Sylvia?"

Sylvia bowed herself over the bronze head at
her knee, and there was distress in her sombre
eyes.

"I wonder if I have done right?" she questioned. "Are you sure you do not mind? are
you very sure? I have taken you away from
your work just when people were beginning to
care and to know. Enid, why did you ever say
you would come with me?"

"You know the reason why, and it is the best
of all reasons; the most valid, the supreme reason. Because I — because I wanted to. We
have talked this over so fully and so many times.
You are tired to-night; that is why you come
back to it. Besides, you are not taking me away
from it;" she stopped a moment, and her face
was fixed and solemn; "nothing ever takes me
away from it. You are helping to fit me for it.
You are broadening my mind. One gets to
thinking that the principles which apply in one's
own town apply to the universe, and one grows
autocratic and insists upon enforcing them. That
is narrow-mindedness and ignorance. I realized
it with a shock to-night. I 've come upon an

entirely new set of conditions, and — I don't exactly tremble for my principles, but I feel much more modest about them than I ever did before. You must regard yourself in the light of a rescuer."

Enid's eyes laughed, but Sylvia's, which had been scanning her face intently, still looked troubled.

"And, moreover," Enid continued, "I do just luxuriate in all this romance and quaintness. I love doing my hair before an ancient pier-glass, and listening to languid young men sing sentimental love-songs. It is like reading light literature because one's doctor prescribes it, and I do adore light literature when my conscience allows me to indulge in it."

Sylvia's face grew even less reassured, and she turned it away absently. Enid went on hastily, feeling the mistake in her own tone.

"Besides, you know when one is actively working, as I was all last winter and this summer, one doesn't get time to take in new ideas; one works the old ones threadbare; and one is in danger of falling behind the times, and losing one's hold on the cause one has been desiring to support. I know I need time for reflection, and if you hadn't carried me off I should never have taken the time. And there are so many things I ought to read. I always feel myself a sham when I think of the way I have been lecturing

on Social Science all winter, and the assurance
with which I have expounded my views, and
when I realize how little I know and how much
I ought to know. It is only because socialistic
and social-scientific ideas are new, and very little
understood by the world in general, that I have
been tolerated at all. But," staring reflectively
at the floor, "I do think I know more than most
of the people I have lectured to; so — perhaps
— it was excusable in me to talk. And now,
when I think of how the bottom of my trunk is
lined with fat books!" Enid paused to bring
to her imagination that delightful picture — "I
rejoice in thinking how wise and well-equipped
I shall be when I go back. And then, too, I
shall be able to test my principles in this entirely
new environment." She twisted a little in order
to look into Sylvia's half-averted face. "Have
faith, dear; it is all for the best. We should
never have come here, if it had not been well to
come."

She was aware, after she had said it, that her
last remark was of rather too passive an optimism
to bring much comfort to a self-accusing soul.

Sylvia sighed, the faintest little sigh, and lay
back in her chair, and the two sat silent for
a while. Enid glanced up questioningly once at
the pale, still face above her, and then looked
towards the clock upon the mantel-shelf, but put
down her head again without saying anything.

"Go to bed, dear," said Sylvia at last; "it is getting late. I am not ready to sleep quite yet, truly. Don't insist upon it. All this newness of place and people has waked me up. But I shall not sit up much longer. I promise."

"I shall do your hair first," replied Enid, getting up.

"Ah, no!" Sylvia cried. "Please not. I did not bring you here to be a maid and to wait upon me."

"No, you were wise not to," returned Enid: "you would have had to discharge me within a week for insubordination;" and she selected the brush and comb from among the toilet articles on the bureau and advanced towards the back of the armchair, brandishing them with determination.

"You humiliate me when you perform these menial services for me," protested Sylvia, with a final attempt at displeasure.

"You humiliate me when you talk about menial services," replied Enid with mocking gravity; "I should think you ought to have derived more profit from my socialistic instruction."

She passed the comb through Sylvia's dark, soft hair, and one or two downy rings fell back again upon the transparent forehead, veined blue at the temples.

"Now," she continued, "I am going to brush out all the hauntings of that large-nosed young man. This is no time of night for him to be

around here puzzling you with his personality.
As for the look in his eyes, I don't believe it
goes back any farther than the retina; but I will
make one concession, — he can sing! I do not
think I ever heard quite such a voice. It was
not powerful, but how sweet! And did you hear
the wail in it, or rather under it?"

Sylvia did not answer, and Enid, accustomed
to her silences, went on: —

"He did not say one word, but the other young
man was quite a chatterer, was n't he? And
such good English! not a bit of an accent; and
such a nice, hearty voice! I liked him, he seemed
so sensible. And did you notice how affectionate
he was with the pretty sister? He looked so
proud when he introduced her. The idea of a
child like that making such music! She must be
a genius. Oh, Sylvia, I am glad we are here!
And it will be a very good place for accomplish-
ing all the reading I ought to do, and you know
I want to write that article for the ' North American.' Shall I braid it in one braid to-night?
Yes, I think I will."

Enid glanced at the clock as she talked.

"I should n't be a bit surprised if we were the
last ones up in this house," she resumed, after
she had separated the hair into three strands.
"At any rate, I am certain that Madame Dumarais is fast asleep. Did you see how funny
she looked, and how bewildered, when her son

introduced us? I know she had been napping
all through that lovely ballad. I saw the young
singer down in the courtyard awhile ago. I went
out on the piazza to explore. Did you know that
our rooms opened out on a broad piazza inclosed
by blinds? Well, they do. Madame Dumarais
spoke of it as a gallery, and it is just that. I
peeped through the shutters and saw the young
man down in the courtyard. He was smoking
a cigarette. I know that will be a disappointment to you."

"How do you know it was not the other one?"
asked Sylvia, looking amused.

"Because he stood near the arch, and the
shadow of his nose was on the wall. It was unmistakable."

They both laughed in a subdued fashion, and
Enid put the brush and comb back on the bureau.

"I shall give you ten minutes for your prayers,
no longer!" she said; "and then I am coming
back, and you are going to lie down in that bed,
and the light is going to be put out."

When she returned to carry out her intentions,
Sylvia was already lying among the pillows.

' "I think I shall go to sleep in a little while
now," she said. "You really do like it here,
don't you, Enid? And you think you can work
well, don't you? If I thought I was keeping
you from working, I should not let you stay one
moment. It is wrong enough to be useless in

the world one's self; but if I thought I were committing the crime of keeping you from living, too, Enid?"

But Enid had her arms about her, and was saying a great many things very softly in the dark.

CHAPTER V

JACQUES' SISTER

"This is my winter!" Jeanne had said one morning at the breakfast-table, as she opened the invitation to her first dancing-party; and afterwards, when the Dumarais and their Northern visitors looked back, they always called the time "Jeanne's winter," and they remembered Jeanne as she flitted through it, ecstatic, startled, delicately lovely.

When the shyness had worn off, — as much as Jeanne's shyness ever did wear off, — she used to run in often upon Enid and Sylvia, crying: —

"Here is another invitation! That makes the third this morning! It is a tea. Jacques is going to get me a book for my engagements. Will it not be a joke? Veritably, grande dame!"

Or there would be a smothered knock, and she would tumble into the room with her arms full of half-unwrapped fluffiness and ribbons.

"See! for the german! And there are to be slippers to match, but they have not arrived. You shall see them."

And perhaps madame had followed her and

would remain standing in the doorway, swaying
like an elephant. Now madame, who had no
taste whatever in decorating her house, was without reproach where the dressing of her daughter
was concerned; and Jacques, with his usual common sense, saw it, and in this one matter accorded her complete authority. No other act of
forbearance on his part could have so stirred the
depths of his step-mother's affection, but this
one aroused in her pathetically humble soul something that was almost adoration. During that
winter, madame experienced more of heaven upon
earth than is permitted to most people. She
ruminated at shop windows and she pored over
fashion-books. Enid and Sylvia did not get very
well acquainted with her, — nobody ever did get
very well acquainted with madame.

"The real festivities do not begin until after
Christmas, you know," Jeanne had explained
gravely to Enid one day soon after the arrival
of the two women. Enid was sitting in Sylvia's
room with one of the fat books on her knees, and
Sylvia was lying on the lounge. They had come
in from a short walk among the narrow French
streets. The weather was close and damp, and
there was no sunlight in the square, plain room.
Sylvia was as white and apathetic as the day itself.

"Do you like balls?" asked Jeanne anxiously.
She sat at the foot of the bed, with her arms
twined upward about one of the posts and her

head inquiringly sidewise.   One foot dangled back and forth.

Sylvia looked at Enid with an amused smile, and Enid laughed as if something were a joke, and said: —

"Oh, of course!   We adore them!"

Jeanne felt reassured.   "Jacques said you would adore them," she announced with a sigh of satisfaction.

"Your brother is evidently very wise about women," returned Enid, but the irony in her tone was lost upon the little French girl.

"Jacques is not my brother," she said; "Jocelin is my brother.   Monsieur Dumarais, my father, married maman when I was a very little girl.   My name is Castaigne."

She was not aware of any inconsistency or lack of clearness in her explanation, but Enid turned the words over in her mind a moment before she said: —

"Ah!" and then, "but he is just like a brother to you, after all, a very nice brother."

"That is what every one says," Jeanne agreed quietly, "but I have not been able to observe that it is true."

Enid's eyes met Sylvia's in a seemingly absent manner.   Jeanne swung her foot, and watched the two friends with the direct, meditative gaze of a child.

"Come over here by me, Jeanne," said Sylvia

after a pause. "I am going to call you Jeanne,
if you will let me; it is such a pretty name, I
like to say it."

"Oh, pray! I shall be charmed!" cried
Jeanne, blushing; and she came and sat down
beside the lounge.

"Tell me," Sylvia continued, "did you make
the little song I heard you singing this morning?"

"Which one?" asked Jeanne, "this?" She
hummed the words and the melody under her
breath: —

> "Vous désirez savoir de moi
> D'où me vient pour vous ma tendresse ;
> Je vous aime, voici pourquoi :
> Vous ressemblez à ma jeunesse."

"That one? Yes, I did the music, but it is
Sully Prudhomme again. It is a song that'
Jacques likes."

"Will you let me see the music of your songs
some day?" asked Sylvia.

"See it?" Jeanne repeated. "But there is
nothing to see!"

"The notes, I mean. I should like to see how
you do it. I have never known any one before
who wrote music."

"Oh!" said Jeanne, and she laughed. "But
I never write it! I only play it on the piano
and sing it as it comes out. How funny that
you thought I wrote it!"

"But, child," gasped Enid, laying the fat book face down on her knee, "you must write it! Why, what are you thinking of?"

Jeanne looked bewildered. "It is not necessary," she explained; "Jocelin learns them in a short while as I play, and I know them already. They remain."

"But only think," said Sylvia, "how many other people might hear them and love them, and sing them too, if you would write them down."

"But I do not know how to do that," Jeanne replied, "and it is just as well, after all, for Jocelin does not care to have other people sing his songs."

"Do you mean to tell me that, with all those music-thoughts stirring in your brain, you have lived for nineteen years and never wanted to make people listen to them?" said Enid. "Does not something cry out within you, ' Come, hear me ' ? "

"I do not know what you mean," said Jeanne, without enthusiasm.

If she had been a stone wall, she could not have proved more stubborn, more inelastic upon encounter; and yet there she sat, poised as lightly as a flower, courteously, uninterestedly expectant. The baby yellowness had never faded from her hair; her eyes were brownest brown, just as they used to be; but she had grown tall, and was made up of long, youthful curves.

Enid, not yet recovered from the shock of the stone wall, stared at this slender, flexile creature. Sylvia, too, had risen on her elbow. All the inherent and trained New Englandism in the two women stood forth amazed, outraged. To their two minds, that, in however widely different ways, were used to hoard and husband every talent jealously, — were used to work their little allotments of appointed or mistaken vocation with never-flagging conscientiousness, harvesting rocks in fortitude and patience year after year, — this light dallying with a great gift was incomprehensible, this irresponsible laziness seemed a crime.

"Don't you know what ambition is?" asked Enid, when she had found her voice.

Jeanne pursed up her lips thoughtfully. She had been thinking of something else, and it was difficult to remember the connection of this question with what had gone before.

"Jacques is ambitious," she replied; "he has told me so."

Enid felt baffled, but she leaned forward and took the girl's hand in her own.

"Look at me. Say this to yourself now, if you have never said it before, which seems incredible to me. Say this: ' I can write songs, I can make music if I will, I can do what the great masters have done, I can create melody. Some day all the world shall listen when my

thoughts speak, shall listen as it does to the great
ones.   I will make it listen!'   Dream! — dream
it, child, if you cannot reason!   Say to yourself,
'If it might be that, after I am dead long years,
my name, like theirs, shall bring a glow to the
heart of every man who hears it!'   You do not
know how to praise God till you have thought
such things."

"It is through such stirrings, too, such knowledge of greatness, that God teaches us humility,"
murmured Sylvia; "the one awakens the other.
It is strange that it should be so."

"The one ought to awaken the other; I believe it was meant to," assented Enid; "but I
do not think it always does, — at least, history
does not show that it does."

They were silent, letting their thoughts travel
along this side issue; but Jeanne brought them
back to the subject in hand.

"I do not understand why you expect me to
take pleasure in thinking about after I am dead,"
she questioned.   "I really should not take pleasure in it.   How could I?"

Enid laughed in spite of herself.   "Think,
then, of the joy of living and creating beautiful
melody!   You played something the other night,
Jeanne, that might have been part of an Orato-
rio.   Think what it means to be given the right
to consecrate your life to the perfecting of a great
art!   Don't you want to do that?"

"I do not find it attractive," said Jeanne apologetically; "but I do not doubt that it might be so for any one who liked it," she added with elaborate politeness.

Nobody seemed to be able to say anything for some time after this. Enid bent the leaves of her book abstractedly, and Sylvia lay with her eyes closed. It is to be doubted whether, five years later, Enid could have taken the trouble to make this appeal to Jeanne's ambition; she might have learned by that time to be skeptical of genius, and ambition, too. But, as yet, she and Sylvia and Jeanne were all young together, after their various fashions. These Northerners were college-bred, and a college woman is invariably younger than other women of her own age. She has been accorded four years more of experiment, of freedom from responsibility, — in a word, of girlhood. She has not been surprised into matrimony, nor huddled out upon the thick of the struggle for existence. She enters the battle armed with a maturity of power and a naïveté of inexperience which make her curiously valiant and impetuous.

A ray of sunshine came through the gallery shutters and lay, barred and wintry pale, upon the threshold of the open door. Down in the courtyard madame's mocking-bird whistled. Sylvia opened her eyes and smiled at Jeanne.

"I have remained too long," said Jeanne timidly; "I have wearied you by talking. You should have sent me away."

"Oh, no, indeed!" said Sylvia reassuringly. "I love to have you. Do not go."

But Jeanne was not to be persuaded. As she went along the gallery she sang the last stanza of the song Jacques liked: —

> "Je vous tends chaque jour la main,
> Vous offrant l'amour qui m'oppresse,
> Mais vous passez votre chemin,
> Vous ressemblez à ma jeunesse."

Enid got up and walked around the room. She moved with a slow, swinging step, and yet softly, and she picked up and set down the small objects on the mantel-shelf and bureau in a restless manner that belied the deliberation of her tread.

"I could not have believed such a thing possible," she said at last. "I did not know talent ever came without also the desire to perfect its expression. Her music is exquisite, and she has no more care for it than if it were a tin trumpet."

"It is something to be released from the desire," said Sylvia huskily; "never to want, and want, at the same time doing nothing."

"I do not believe that there is release from the desire," said Enid gravely; "one must be born without it, — otherwise it remains." She stood beside the lounge and looked down. "When you are well, you will no longer do nothing."

"Shall I not?" whispered Sylvia. "What is 'well'? Something is wrong with me, for I have never known."

This was a mood that Enid had schooled herself to endure, but a look of discouragement crossed her face as she pushed a chair to the side of the lounge and sat down.

"Sylvia," she began gently, "don't you think it is a little foolish in you to talk about never having done things, when you have gone through four years of college life and taken your degree?"

"And how?" asked Sylvia, with a choke in her voice. "Dragging constantly along the edge of a breakdown. Never ready with a paper when it was due, always asking longer time, always leaving a thing with a sense that it was unfinished, because I could see how much better it would have been if I had done it another way; at the end, just catching at the vanishing edges of that degree. How they ever gave it to me I can't imagine! I always feel ashamed to own it. It was because I was so young then that the mere fact of staying there gave me hope. Was it fair to lure me on by such a miserable half-achievement and then drop me flat, doing nothing? Sometimes I get to the point where I can't sentimentalize over divine Love and Justice any longer. I trust it is an occasional relief to God. If you want to comfort me, Enid, don't bring back those weary college days."

"Oh, Sylvia!" said Enid; "Oh, Sylvia!"

"No, dear, no! I did not mean just that. I did not mean the part that belongs to you, — to you and me. I forgot! It is the happiest time in my life when I look back."

Sylvia laughed tearfully at her own inconsistency, and Enid smiled.

"Then we won't consider college an achievement," she said; "we'll consider all the money you've spent on me and my schemes since you've known me. It seems to me most people would regard the establishment of a crèche by day and a reading-room by night as something of an achievement. And think of the deserving and undeserving poor that I have trailed up to your door to receive food and five-dollar bills!"

"No! don't make me think of that!" whispered Sylvia. "The activity of other people presses on me like a mountain sometimes and stifles me. It was none of my doing, all that; it was yours, and you know it. The world is so busy, and watching it drains away my power to do anything."

Enid felt desperate. The doctors had said of Sylvia: "There is no organic disease. Take her to an entirely new environment. Try to rouse her out of her timidity and irresolution without making her conscious that she is being roused." But that was the difficulty. Sylvia's mind was discouragingly wide awake and suspicious; she always divined when you were trying to approach her off her mental guard. This abnormal sensitiveness, which was in the beginning one of the causes of her nervous prostration, was also, in its aggravated form, a result of the disease and complicated the cure.

"Get her interested in something without letting her know it," the doctors said. "Get her outside of her own mind. If she could think without considering the fact that she was thinking, she would be on the road to recovery."

And Enid left her lectures and classes, resigned from her committees, gave up her scheme of spending the winter in a model tenement, and came, as Sylvia's guest, to New Orleans. She had an unsatisfied theory that friendship must work regeneration; she did not call it regeneration when she thought of it, because she would never have acknowledged, even to herself, that Sylvia needed regenerating, but that was what her theory meant to her. And, watching the invalid day after day, her heart ached as she recognized that even the strong friendship between them failed to touch the mainspring of Sylvia's life and set her will in motion. Enid rebelled against this thought, which was hardly a thought as yet, — only an undefined dread. She did not believe it was going to be true. She did not see how it ever could be true. She refused to have it so.

As a woman advances towards thirty unmarried, her women-friendships possess more and more a stability, an intensity, which were lacking in the explosively sentimental intimacies of her youth; they are to her instead of many things. And as she passes into the region of the middleaged, and the world grows more and more workaday, she may become self-conceited and self-gratulatory enough about her work, but she will thank God for her friends. We all want to mean something to somebody, and the friendships of a single woman satisfy to her this desire, — except in certain moods.

Enid averred once that, with a married woman, husband and children, the particular, the personal relationships, must come first, but that the unmarried woman, who consecrates herself to a cause deliberately, gives up the personal claims; it is a part of the sacrifice. Shortly after making this statement, Enid came South with Sylvia. She sat by the couch now, and her face was grave and insistent.

"You know I shall always believe that you can do what you would, if you will," she said.

Sylvia moved uneasily, and turned her eyes away; she did not contradict, she did not say anything. And Enid, remorseful, searched her mind for a change of subject that should not be too obvious and abrupt. Presently she said in a lighter tone: —

"I fear the true explanation of the abortion of Jeanne's ambition is simply that she is swayed by another emotion which is more powerful. She evidently did not care to regard Monsieur Jacques in the light of a brother, did you notice? Such a very uninteresting person to fall in love with, too! Nice, noisy, self-sufficient young man, but without a particle of romance about him."

"Poor Monsieur Jacques!" said Sylvia. "So the fiat has gone forth against him, and he is labeled ' commonplace '? "

"I wonder if he is in love with her," mused Enid; "he'd be a delightful person to go out and buy furniture with; he would always be able to get the proper per cent. off. He could drive nails and hang pictures beautifully, but I wonder if he can make love? Dear me! what is happening to me that I sit up here in broad daylight, and gossip about love and matrimony like a sentimental girl of seventeen, when I ought to be reading Socialism? It is something in the atmosphere of this place. I shall hold you responsible for my degeneration, Sylvia Bennett."

Of course she wished the next minute that she had n't said it. She was wishing twenty times a day that she had n't said things, but this once she was relieved from embarrassing protests by a hurry and flutter along the gallery, a hasty knock, and the entrance of Jeanne with cards.

Jeanne watched the reception of the cards with

the excited constraint of one who has been party
to the lighting of a fuse, and now expects a sensation.

"Miss Campion," read Sylvia aloud, without
enthusiasm.

"Miss Campion," repeated Enid, gazing at her
card in the stolid and impartial fashion of one
who knows not that she is being favored of gods
and men.

"It must be one of the people Cousin Jessie
wrote about," said Sylvia. "She insisted on
asking two or three to call."

"She is very important," cried Jeanne, tumbling over her words, and not yet realizing that
her audience had failed to be impressed. "She
is very important, and rich and beautiful. She
has l'air grande dame, tout parfait. Jacques has
dined at her house. She does not marry, but
everybody falls in love with her."

Enid felt an unworthy desire to test Jeanne by
asking if "everybody" included Jacques, but of
course she did not do so.

"I suppose we shall have to go down," said
Sylvia in a bored tone, sitting up on the lounge
and lifting her hands to her hair.

"I suppose so," acquiesced Enid with a sigh,
and the leaves of the fat book came together with
an impatient whack.

"Thank you, Jeanne."

CHAPTER VI

ROMA CAMPION CALLS

THEY found out in the short half hour of her
visit that she was a worldly woman, ambitious,
traveled, fastidious, and discontented. They
suspected that she was ignorant and indifferent
in socialistic and industrial matters, and that she
possessed a steady, painstaking, unintellectual
mind. They knew she was, in many ways, the
kind of woman they most disapproved of, and
they fell in love with her on the spot.

On her own part she was, from the first, attracted towards them. They represented the
type of woman which she respected most, knew
least, and was curious to know better, — the type
upon whose model she felt the least courage,
and it may be the least intellectual ability, to
conform her own life. Aside from this general
impression, which she had really gained beforehand from the letter Sylvia's cousin had written,
she recognized that they were also interesting as
individuals. She was quicker at understanding
human nature than she was at understanding
books, — that is, to put it differently, she might

not always comprehend a joke, but she could comprehend thoroughly the man who made the joke. It was chiefly instinct, of course, — natural inclination; otherwise she could never have been what she was, the brilliant society woman, — as the cant phrase has it, — the envy, the despair, the adoration of her world, in whatsoever geographical part of it she chose to shine. But her insight was partly due to training as well: she had been in the world, and, to a considerable extent, of the world, all her life; whereas she had been taught to use books as polite accessories of the social art, — well-bred means of passing the time and of making conversation.

Enid and Sylvia had never before believed that they could have anything in common with the self-confessed society woman. Occasionally, in their youth, and after their relatives had laid before them, with more than ordinary emphasis, the social exigencies of that station in life to which they were called, they would reluctantly array themselves and sally forth in weariness and trepidation of spirit to what they were pleased to designate contemptuously as "a function;" but these concessions to family tradition were few, and for days after their occurrence they darkened, as with a nightmare hideousness, the minds of Enid and Sylvia. For the words "sociable" and "socialistic" are not synonymous. Of late years, however, "the function" — which, in bald language, meant to them anxious patronage by a busy hostess, palpable neglect on the part of the young male contingent, and indifference, or half-amused contempt from the popular girls — had abated its terrors. This was due, as far as Sylvia was concerned, to the excuse which her ill-health afforded her for refusing invitations, and, in the case of Enid, to her gradual recognition and adoption by the sprinkling of the learned and the lionized who saw fit to frequent, and even at times to enjoy, the entertainments provided by their well-meaning but less enlightened brethren. Society had therefore become for both women an institution which they were willing to tolerate, but not to admire; and, while they continued to evince a languid and somewhat melancholy interest in those of their college friends who had drifted into this orthodox way of life, they fought shy of society women in general.

To-day, however, they had talked to one of these women for half an hour with animated friendliness and distinct enjoyment. The talk had been of that rapid, desultory sort which results upon a first meeting between people who feel immediate friendliness for one another, and which is like nothing so much as a continuous striking of sparks. The transition from subject to subject is swift and unconscious; the minds click against each other at every instant and pour forth their thoughts breathlessly, in their haste to prove affinity upon as many points as possible, and thereby justify to themselves this sudden and incautious surrender to impulse. A great deal of conversation can be made in half an hour, if there are no pauses. Moreover, Enid, for one, had, among the reporters who tried to take down her lectures, a reputation for talking with exceptional rapidity.

From the weather the talk floated on to the town itself; from the town to its society, to society in general; then, of course, — for was not Enid there? — to the regeneration of society, to the literary propaganda on social questions, to literature itself, to literary people, to amateurism, to dilettanteism, and so back to society. Just where the transitions came, no one stopped to consider.

It was Roma Campion who, in the mysterious fashion best known to herself, eliminated at the outset all stiffness, all constraint, from the interview, saying her tentative and tactful social nothings in her unobtrusive, well-bred voice, and looking at her hearer straight the while with deference and interest. Long afterwards Enid concluded that the unquenchable sincerity looking out of this worldly woman's eyes was the beginning and the end of the fascination. But that first day Enid did not stop to analyze the fascination; she caught up the small-talk at its

first rebound, and carried it forward in a flood of
eloquence, transformed and dignified.

And Sylvia, vibrating beside her, — Sylvia, the
shy, the reserved, the silent, — interrupted again
and again, speaking almost eagerly. At the last
the right of speech drifted back to Miss Campion, and she invited the two to dine with her
and go to the opera the next week, and, standing
at the parlor door, she railed a little, albeit with
that restraint and coolness which the occasion
required, against the dullness and self-compla-
cency of her native town. And as they stood on
the shallow stairs behind the open glass door and
watched her go down the passage to her carriage,
which all this while had been quite a serious
obstacle in the narrow street, Enid and Sylvia
felt for this woman, slightly older than themselves and already scarred and embittered by the
experience of her own folly, a tenderness and
enthusiasm which their judgment told them was
wholly out of proportion to their knowledge of
her character and her deserts.

And she, leaning back among her cushions,
was less bored by life than she had been since
she left Paris in October. Her world would
have been slow to acknowledge that Roma Campion was capable of enthusiasms; it would have
laughed at even a hint of such a thing; it would
have changed "enthusiasms" into "fads," and felt
that it was displaying considerable knowledge of

human nature. But Miss Campion was unusually preoccupied as she drove home. She made no attempt to recognize acquaintances, and this was not her custom. She did not even bow to Curtis Baird as he passed her, swinging along beside young Dumarais, with whom he was going home to dine *en famille*, and she had been peculiarly gracious to Curtis Baird ever since he had presented his letter of introduction.

"My lady is in a brown study," he thought, but he said nothing, as Jacques was talking of other things.

The Dumarais' dinner-table was a noisy one that day. Jacques, by some more than usually clever business transaction, had been able to make himself appear particularly valuable in the eyes of his firm; and the knowledge that he could, if he chose, assert his independence and withdraw altogether on the first of January filled his soul with glee.

"And did you go to the cathedral?" he asked Enid, his gray eyes and white teeth flashing a charming smile.

He liked Enid. She did not burden him with a sense of responsibility. It was still an astonishment to him that she obviously never expected him to make an effort to entertain her, but it was a relief as well. He did not know that he entirely approved this frank though unspoken avowal that the attentions of his sex were matters

of complete indifference to her; it was not quite
in accord with his ideas of feminine modesty;
but, after all, it was convenient when a man
came home tired and hungry after a hard day's
work.

"How have you amused yourself?" he continued, prolonging his friendly smile.

"We did not go to the cathedral this time,"
she answered; "we waited for a brighter day.
Your sister took us to the place where the Italians were murdered, Congo Square, — was it
Rampart Street?"

"'Murdered' is good!" observed Jacques,
turning upon Enid a mocking but provokingly
genial countenance.

He irritated her, he was always so self-confi-
dent. Sylvia threw her a timid, warning glance
across the table; and Curtis Baird let his chin
sink against his throat, and looked out at her
smilingly from under his drooped eyelids.

"What term would you substitute?" inquired
Enid.

"When a band of ruffians has murdered the
chief of police, citizens find themselves looking
at law and order from a new point of view. I
should say 'righteously executed'!" Jacques declared with stern emphasis. His chin was very
square.

"Oh, — come, — now, — Dumarais! you would
n't, — would you?" interrupted Mr. Baird in the

quietest of slow, conversational tones. " Think of the time it takes — to say — all — that, ' right-eously — exe-cut-ed ' ! Invent something shorter, — can't you? Think what it would mean — to — do — all — that, if a man had — an impediment in his speech."

"Perhaps you would prefer ' murdered ' also?" said Jacques, lifting his eyebrows to the height of their interrogatory possibilities, and speaking with a good-nature that might have been considered alarmingly crisp.

"No, — I should n't," replied Baird reflectively; "it — is n't a — pretty — word, — ' murdered.' I should — feel — quite — grateful — on behalf of the — language, if you — could — supply — a better one."

Mr. Baird's drawl was by no means the least of his many attractions, ladies said, and they usually added that he had affected it so long, it had ceased to be an affectation. His words were like a string of disconnected freight-cars left to slide along a track through their own momentum, and coupling at unexpected intervals.

"No! but seriously, you know," began Jacques, "it was n't murder. They were guilty, and they knew it, and everybody knew it, and they deserved all they got. Why! they attacked that man from behind! "

"Then why did the law acquit them?" It was Enid this time, speaking indignantly.

"Ah! — well!" Jacques' tone and shrug implied that, if you were going to ask him to justify the idiosyncrasies of the law, of course there was no use carrying the discussion any farther.

"You feel that the action was justifiable, then?" Enid resumed after a pause, which had been eloquent of disapproval.

"Justifiable!" exclaimed Jacques. He was not angry, you know; he was only French. "Justifiable! Well, I should rather think! Why, my dear young lady, there wasn't a man in this town that would have dared to call his soul his own twenty-four hours afterwards if we hadn't done it. The beggars were so elated, they were ready to murder us in our beds without compunction, every mother's son of us! Yes, I mean it!" he continued, smiling cheerfully once more in response to Enid's unspoken skepticism.

"Then I don't see, if everybody knew they were guilty, why they didn't hang them," she said.

"That's just what we did do, as soon as we got a chance!" vociferated Jacques. "We took them out and shot them and strung them up, and then we went home."

"But it wasn't law," insisted Enid.

"Maybe it wasn't," retorted Jacques, "but it was justice. Have I got to stand by a law when it is a rotten law? Have I got to submit to a

court decision that's bought up and paid for?
Have I got to bow down to a department of judi-
ciary that's so bribed and corrupted and intimi-
dated it hasn't a leg of its own to stand on?
No! because, if I have, I'll move out! When a
law can't be enforced, something's wrong, and
it's time for a change. All change comes as an
upsetting of law. There never was a change yet
that wasn't called unlawful by the old fogies.
But are we all to stand still on that account, and
never advance? Are we to stifle in our own cor-
ruption? I say there's something higher in this
world than what we call law!"

He paused, stared fiercely at his antagonist,
and then, with a sudden change of expression,
beamed upon her indulgently.

"I beg your pardon!" he said heartily, half
laughing; "I forgot I wasn't talking to a man.
I pounded it down rather hard, but you see, not
being a conservative myself, I don't look at
things in just your way."

To have her own radical generalizations thus
cast upon her head, and to be herself catalogued
as a conservative, was a new experience for Enid,
and it took her a moment to rally from the shock.

"You'll — find him an — awful radical, Miss
Spenser," said Baird slowly, with an alluring
twinkle under his eyelashes; "regular — fire-eater
— Jacques is."

Down at the end of the table old Monsieur

Dumarais turned his ear towards the speaker with a suspicious frown, but Enid only half heard the words, and Jacques did not see the twinkle.

"Are n't your assertions a little beside the question, Mr. Dumarais?" Enid had gathered together her scattered senses and returned to the charge. "You mistake me when you call me a conservative. I, too, believe what you have just said about change and bad laws. But in this case it does not seem to have been the law which was at fault. If the law had been kept, there would have been no disturbance, at least as I see it; but your citizens first broke the law by lending themselves to bribery and intimidation, and then broke it again by having resource to mob rule and bloodshed. That appears to me to be the case by your own presentation of the facts."

"And because we 've made one mistake, you 'd have us keep right on and make another?" said Jacques. "Because we were weak enough, some of us, to be bribed to bring in a verdict of not guilty, when we knew we were perjuring ourselves, you 'd have the rest of us, who were n't such cowards, calmly sit down and let several murderers be turned loose on the community?"

"I do not see but that it would have been perfectly just for you to have suffered the consequences of that first mistake." Enid spoke with deliberation, because she was not altogether sure of herself.

"And how about the murderers suffering for their behavior?" Jacques demanded.

"Conscience, you know, Dumarais, — don't forget the — power — of conscience," said Baird, with elaborate solemnity. "Remorse, — that — sort of — thing. Great factor, — conscience!"

"Great humbug!" retorted Jacques.

"It seems to me, by that first mistake you voluntarily abandon the right to deal with the murderers," said Enid.

"Well, as a matter of theory, my dear lady, perhaps we do, but you'll find this world isn't all a matter of theory; and practical necessity isn't going to let any man see the feasibility of having a murderer running around the streets, no matter how many mistakes he has made in letting that murderer - get there. We did it then, and we'd do it again to-morrow, every man of us, and not turn a hair."

Jacques, having thus strangled the argument by violence, in this brutal appeal to fact, laid his knife and fork parallel upon his plate and gazed around the table with a complacent air of victory. He thought he had gained his point, as no doubt he had to a certain extent, if silence can be called the end of an argument. And Enid, moved by the distress in Sylvia's eyes, let him think so.

"But it was an impressive sight!" he said. Having established the validity of his case, to his own satisfaction, he was now ready to describe it in its dramatic character as an incident in history. "I was n't there when they did the killing "—

"Come, — come, — Dumarais, — stand up — for your colors! Don't be timid, — man, — you 're among friends!" said Baird, with the inevitable drawl. "I have n't found a fellow — yet — who was there — at the — time — of the — killing."

"Well, I was n't, this time! No fooling, Baird. I know it 's not often I 'm not on hand, but this is honest truth."

Mr. Baird persisted in looking incredulous.

"I got there just about ten minutes after it was done, and you may not believe it, but there was hardly any one left around that place. They dispersed like magic. One of the Italians was hanging against a tree, dead. He had long hair, and, I give you my word, that hair was standing up all over his head, and the ends were waving to and fro in the wind. It was an awful sight!"

A shiver went around the table.

"Were you there?" asked Sylvia of Jocelin, who sat next to her and attended to her wants assiduously, but was not talkative.

"No, mademoiselle," he answered, "I was not here last winter, last year."

"Why is he so silent?" she thought; "is he timid, or unhappy?"

He had made a few courteous responses to

questions at the beginning of the meal, but had remained quiet during the discussion, attentive, for the most part, to his plate, but glancing up with some show of interest when Enid's remarks had proved particularly exasperating to his stepbrother. Sylvia found him more difficult of approach than the other members of the family. Her own timidity kept her from at once breaking down the barrier of reverent silence behind which he persistently intrenched himself. His position in the household puzzled her, for whereas Jacques departed each morning punctually at half past eight, and was no more seen till dinner-time, Jocelin came and went irregularly. Sometimes at two o'clock in the afternoon he was playing an accompaniment on the piano in the parlor, and at any time of day he might be found walking about the courtyard smoking a cigarette. Sunday morning Sylvia inferred from his appearance that he had been out before breakfast, and he ate rapidly, excused himself before the meal was over, and went out again. Jeanne had said, "This is Jocelin's busy day," and madame had looked less careworn than she usually did when Jocelin had engagements which took him away from the house.

Sylvia had never before met any man who was so considerate of her comfort. Now it was a door he closed; again he was suggesting that she might enjoy the fire more if she sat in this other chair. So deft was he in his unobtrusiveness that even Enid, the watchful, did not notice what he was about. But Sylvia could not fail to see, since the little attentions were meant for her. There was a personal and caressing quality in his manner of setting a chair for her which was as insistent in its demand for recognition as were his gentleness and the lonely look in his eyes.

The dessert was on the table, and Jacques was still describing the putting down of the Italians.

"That afternoon and the next day they were getting out of town like ants pouring out of an ant-hill. When they couldn't afford to go by train, they walked along the railroad tracks. They say it was a sight to see them back of town. It was the only thing to do, and we did it!" he ended, as if finally closing the subject.

Enid remained silent. Another item came to Jacques' mind, and he began again:—

. "They say that women, ladies even, went down after it was over, to see the place, and, if possible, the men before they were taken down."

"Oh, no!" cried Sylvia; "not ladies!"

"I don't know," returned Jacques with a shrug; "I only heard. Curiosity is by no means the least charming characteristic of your sex, mademoiselle. I did not let Jeanne go, for example, but it was said they even went down in carriages."

He dwelt on his information with a teasing

smile, and spoke in a politely bantering tone. He saw that the remarks made his guests indignant, and, as one of them had pushed him rather closely in the foregoing argument, he was not sorry to tease her a little.

The word "carriages" brought to Enid's mind Miss Campion's well-appointed vehicle. Curtis Baird watched her, despite his assumption of indifference, with some interest. This was an excellent opportunity for her to turn Jacques' implications about the vulgar curiosity of women in general against the women of his own city in particular. Would she see it? If she did, she ignored it, at least directly.

"I met one of your New Orleans women to-day whom I should not think likely to do such a thing," she said quietly.

She was feeling that her own impetuous liking for the woman would be appropriately disciplined if it should transpire that she could do such a thing, after all.

"And may I ask who that was?" said Jacques cordially.

Baird lifted his chin and opened his eyes to their ordinary width this time, as he looked at Enid. He already knew who it was.

"Her name is very odd and pretty," she replied; "Miss Roma Campion."

"Ah!" said Jacques. He turned and looked full upon her for a moment, with more of interest than he had ever shown. "Is that so?" he added, in a tone that seemed to congratulate her; "you are fortunate!"

"And was Miss — Campion — one of those — who went — down to — to see the — remains?" inquired Baird, with more than his customary deliberation.

Jacques threw back his head with a chuckle.

"She wasn't here at the time," he said; "it was early in the fall when it happened, you know; but I should n't venture to be certain of what she might have done if she had been here. It would n't be safe."

Mr. Baird leaned back in his chair and smiled.

"By the way," Jacques continued, "I should n't wonder if she passed us coming from here as we were on our way down to dinner. Seems to me I remember her carriage. Did you notice?"

"Yes, — I noticed," said Baird.

"I was singing in the parlor," said Jeanne eagerly, "and I did not hear her come in, and as I got up to go away she spoke to me."

"What did she say?" asked Jacques.

"She said," — Jeanne was blushing in the prettiest way imaginable, — "she said, ' I am sorry I interrupted your song. You must tell Mr. Dumarais that I do not feel inclined to pardon him for not telling me he had a sister who could give such pleasure by her singing.' Then she held out her hand and looked at me, — but she is adorable, yes! She kept my hand a moment and said, ' I wonder how it is that I have never seen your face? I know I have not, for I must have remembered it.' "

"Ah, ha!" cried Jacques. He looked immensely pleased.

"And I told her, ' I am just out this winter; that may be the reason.' And she said, ' Really! ' as if — as if it were the most interesting news. Is she not beautiful? And then she said, ' I hope it will be a happy winter; I am quite sure it will be.' Ah, but I wished to embrace her! "

Curtis Baird's eyes emitted a flash, and then became once more serenely blue and smiling.

"You may embrace me instead, bébé," laughed Jacques; "you will find me twice as appreciative."

"Decidedly he is not in love with Jeanne," thought Enid; and with much inconsistency, considering her heroic efforts of the afternoon, she added, "poor little thing!"

"I went to school with her two little sisters one year," said Jeanne, "before they went away to France to be finished. They were not very nice. They are to come out together next year; she told me that, too."

The invitation to the opera was mentioned during the evening, and by degrees it dawned upon Enid and Sylvia that, for some reason, as yet but dimly appreciated by themselves, they were being regarded as more than ordinarily blessed among mortals. As individuals they had manifestly increased in importance within the past twelve hours.

Enid was not accustomed to owing her importance to any one but herself. She had not realized before how habituated she had become to the smile of intelligence which at home was certain to greet the mention of her name. The old, familiar "Miss Enid Spenser? Ah, yes! we all know Miss Spenser through her work, — I am most happy," etc., no longer sounded in her ears. There was a blank where this had been, and Enid was disconcerted to find herself noticing this blank, nay, even feeling amazement that it should be there. She held herself at arm's length from herself and taunted her own vanity, but with vexation of spirit. Even this clever Mr. Baird, who came from New York, was apparently at a loss just, how to place her. His manner indicated that he felt she had done something, but he was waiting to find out what that something was. This negative sort of ignorance of her position, however, she could endure, scorning herself for even noticing it. But to be definitely relegated to oblivion, as a conservative, was harder to bear; and to be lifted into importance through the patronage of a woman, whose highest achievements consisted in dressing well and bruising men's hearts, was hardest of all. She was filled with a sharp astonishment, and the sense that the situation was a humorous one did not afford her the consolation which she felt that it ought.

The next day Jacques announced that he, too, had received an invitation to dine with Miss Campion and go to the opera afterwards.

"And so has Baird; so we shall be a jolly party. Do you know I really think Baird is quite gone in that direction? He calls as much as once a week, and she rather singles him out. I've warned him, but of course it's no use. I suppose, if I were in love with a lovely woman, I'd behave just as idiotically as the rest of them."

Jacques swelled his chest, and pursed his lips sarcastically. It was something for a young man of no fortune to be smiled upon by a woman of position and discrimination. It was something, also, to have been able to endure the smile without succumbing to its fascination. Jacques was excusable in feeling that he had cause to congratulate himself.

"I'll see what I can do for Jeanne," he thought. "It might be a very good thing."

As it happened, however, matters arranged themselves without Jacques' assistance. Sylvia had several days of headache and weakness, and was afraid to use up her strength by going to anything so wearisome as a dinner, or so exciting as the opera. Enid, therefore, wrote regretting for her and explaining the situation; and a note

at once came to Jacques from Miss Campion,
asking him if he could bring his sister, and putting the matter in the light of a favor, since
otherwise her dinner must be one-sided. There
were also some graceful expressions of pleasure
in having already met Jeanne and heard her sing.
Nothing could have been more opportune for the
little sister.

"Oh, I am sorry you cannot go!—so very
sorry!" Jeanne cried sympathetically to Sylvia.
"But are n't you glad she has invited me,—oh,
are you not?" She executed an impromptu
dance on the green and red hearth-rug as she
said it.

"Now, my child," said Jacques, with enthusiasm, "live up to this, and you will be the envy
of all the girls."

Jeanne laughed without a particle of malice in
her mind against those other girls. To have
pleased Jacques was quite enough to make any
one happy,—at least so she thought.

"If you will allow me," Jocelin ventured to
say on the night before the eventful one, when
the others were commiserating Sylvia, and wondering if it might not have been possible for her
to go, after all,— "if you will allow me, Miss Bennett, I should be glad to go over the opera music
to-morrow night, if it would amuse you? And
you could follow what they also are enjoying."

"Yes, he's a dear!" Enid assented the next

evening as she bade Sylvia good-by; "and it will be nice to know you are hearing the same things. I shall think of it as I listen. But you mustn't let him keep you up too late. I've noticed that when he begins, he never seems to know when to stop."

CHAPTER VII

SYLVIA GOES TO THE OPERA

THROUGHOUT the day, Sylvia and Jocelin had
made a little joke of their going to the opera that
evening; and when Sylvia came down to dinner
in a pearl-gray gown with the old lace that had
been her mother's, soft and full and high about
her throat, she found at her place three pale
pink roses which Jocelin had gathered from the
rosebush in the courtyard. "For if mademoiselle goes to the opera, assuredly she must have
flowers," he said.

Nor was the dinner as dull an affair as one
might have imagined it must be, with Jacques
the noisy, and Enid the clever, and Jeanne the
merry, away. Ah, no! for Monsieur Dumarais
was easily led to talk of his favorites, Hugo, and
Sully Prudhomme, and Leconte de Lisle. And
he was one who talked with the taste of the poets'
thoughts upon his lips. Madame, too, had made
a little fête, and the dinner was excellent. It
was Jocelin who called attention to the fact that
no one but maman could have imparted such a
delicious flavor to the *sauce piquante*, and by the

time the dessert was placed on the table maman's strawberry gelatine was not more rosy or unstable than she.

After the coffee, monsieur went away to smoke his cigar in his own little study, whose walls were lined with the beloved books that he should never read again. He used to pass his hands over the backs of them on the shelves, as one passes one's hand over the hair of a child. Sometimes, of an evening, he would take down a book and put it back again softly, now this one, now that one, saying to himself in a meditative whisper: —

"This is ' Légendes des Siècles,' second volume; this is de Musset, ' Les Drames.' "

Sometimes he would sit in his armchair for an hour or more with a book laid open upon his knee, and his cigar held carefully out on one side, so that no ashes nor sparks should drop and soil or burn the precious pages. Not a speck of dust was allowed to rest upon those shelves; monsieur had eyes ' in the ends of his fingers,' as the saying goes, and he did his own dusting.

To-night, when he went into the little room, he called out cheerily, "I, too, shall go to the opera this evening; I shall occupy a baignoir; " and he left the door open into the hall.

Perhaps Jocelin forgot about his cigarette this once, for he did not go down into the courtyard. He tinkered at the fire in the parlor until he had made a broad blaze. He turned down the flame of the reading-lamp, — undoubtedly Jocelin had an eye for effect. The old room assumed uncertain, ever-varying dimensions in the leaping light and shadow; the tawdry trimmings sank into darkness, or shot forth momentarily, now and then, as mere shapeless flashes of color. Jocelin's ancestor came and went upon the wall.

Jocelin pushed an armchair and a hassock where Sylvia could look at the fire, and where he, by glancing sidewise from the piano, without turning his head, could look at Sylvia.

"You would like a shawl?" he questioned. "No? Then I think the curtain may rise."

He let his fingers slip along vaguely over the keys for a few moments with the same sort of assurance and nonchalance with which a man accustomed to the water will turn over on his back and float. And the opera had begun.

Madame came in and out with audible caution several times during the early part of the evening, but finally settled down in her chair by the table with "L'Abeille," the newspaper, and went peacefully, and by good fortune noiselessly, to sleep.

The opera was "Rigoletto."

"Of course you know these songs will not be correct, mademoiselle; I can only give you the air, transposed to the range of my own voice."

Jocelin was finding the notes with his fingers as he talked. Sylvia watched him wonderingly while he dawdled over the music. It seemed he was in no hurry to begin. "Tinkle, tinkle, tinkle," said the notes. There was a rambling harmony to this lazy preamble, nothing more. Jocelin was slightly round-shouldered; his head drooped forward, and he looked at the keys with eyes that were full of dreams.

"The world has gone by," thought Sylvia. "It is in a hurry, — let it go!"

Jocelin quickened his pace delicately: —

"Comme la plume au vent, femme varie."

He was beginning with the tenor's song at the wrong end of the opera. He sang it whimsically, somehow, then changed to the soprano solo in the second act; then drifted up and down the piano again, and with a sudden bound was off into the little drinking song, with the "Hupp!" and the uplift at the end.

"Charming!" cried Sylvia; "encore, encore!"

So he sang it again, this time with bewitching abandon, and at the end Sylvia's laugh rippled in and out with the music, up and down the piano, until, with a tragic sweep of octave, he brought the melody round to Rigoletto's song after the betrayal of his daughter, — the gay song with the sobs beneath the laughter, and the grief rending and tearing the flimsy make-believe of light-heartedness. Jocelin dropped his hands from the piano when it was over, and sat still for a moment before he turned and said: —

"Shall we change to something else now?"

Sylvia could only nod. She still saw the pitiful figure of the broken-hearted old clown; she still heard the wail through the choppy "lull-la-la-a" of his song.

"Did Enid hear it sung like that?" she wondered.

"This is ' La Juive,' then," he said, and presently sang the cardinal's song.

"We have the advantage over the other opera people in that we can change our music whenever we choose, and take it backwards or forwards or in the middle," said Sylvia; and he nodded and smiled, still playing.

"O ma fille chérie, O ma fille chérie."

Jocelin paused, lingered on the notes as if he would begin again, and said, while one hand still droned idly over the keys: —

"That duet is a — do you call it milestone? — in my life. When I was a little boy, I was singing it one day, and Jacques came out and told me that his father was going to marry my mother."

There was a short silence. Jocelin still moved his hand upon the keys, but without striking them.

"Yes?" said Sylvia, in a tone that left him free to be silent or to continue.

He chose to continue, and, still with head bent

down and face half turned towards her, but eyes upon his vaguely restless fingers, he said: —

"I was under the bath-house across the lake, and I was singing. I remember it was a gray day, and Jacques came up out of the water and told me that. And — I was only ten years old — I cried. We were not alike: how could he understand? Jacques is very good to my mother, and to my sister, but — we are not congenial; when you say that, it is all said."

He shrugged his shoulders and smiled winningly upon her for a moment, then turned his eyes back to the keys.

"Pardon me, mademoiselle; I will return to the music."

"No, no!" Sylvia hastened to cry out. "At least, — of course, do not talk about it if you do not wish to, but I enjoy hearing you tell of your life; it has grown up in such a different atmosphere from my own, it is as interesting to me as a romance."

So Jocelin twisted around on the piano-stool, and the firelight fell upon his face and sank into his wistful eyes; and, sitting thus, he began to do the thing he knew how to do best, next after his singing, and that was, to talk about himself.

"It is not much of a life," he said quietly; "it is not what I wanted it to be — But that is past now."

He made an interesting figure with his thin,

brown face, and the red, curved lips beneath the small black moustache, and that pathetic droop to his shoulders, as he sat there before the fire, saying these melancholy words. From the bottom of her heart Sylvia pitied him, and this was what he had meant that she should do.

"But you are young," she ventured; "why is it you speak like that?" And as she said it, she thought of her own life; and she, too, was young.

"It is my voice, mademoiselle," he answered; and again, with the quietness that is not sad, but is more sorrowful than sadness, "my voice!"

"Your voice?" she said perplexedly; "I do not understand. It is a very beautiful voice; surely you must know that?"

He shrugged his shoulders half contemptuously, as a child might who was offered one sweetmeat and preferred another.

"When I was a little boy, everybody said, ' He will have a marvelous voice!' When I sang, the ladies wept and embraced me and said, ' You have a future before you, my child.' I did not love anything so much as I loved my voice. I shall never be able to love anything with a greater love. It has always seemed to me that it is presumptuous in me to think that I could love a human being — a woman — with the holiness, the unselfishness, that the word ' love ' means to me. Others claim that they do it, but how can they hope to?"

There was a large humility about these simple
words that made them worthy of being spoken by
a greater saint than Jocelin. His eyes were
those of a pure-hearted child as he looked at
Sylvia. This was the great charm about Jocelin, that he believed every word he said to you,
at the moment that he said it.

"My voice was mine," he went on. "That
was not an unselfish love, but I loved it. And
it has been as a child that grows up full of promise and becomes a disappointment to its father.
But a father always loves his child."

He smiled a whimsical smile that seemed to
ask pardon for his fantastic notion, and continued : —

"You admire my voice, mademoiselle, — you
think it is remarkable, and large, and sufficient
to satisfy any one. That is because I know how
to use it so well."

He said this without the faintest shade of self-
conceit in voice or manner, and indeed he felt
none; he was merely stating a fact.

"I have had excellent training. I believe I
know how to do with my voice whatever can be
done with it, but as a matter of fact it contains
only about eight notes. It is a baritone, and
a baritone of short range. About eight notes I
have; the rest is what we in French call *factice*.
It is a trick. I am able to make you think I do
things which in reality I do not do at all. Because

I have learned the art of singing, and because
I know my voice, I can do this. In addition, I
have no volume. You have heard me sing in
a parlor, mademoiselle. If you were to hear me
sing in the opera house " — He stopped, and
his sensitive mouth contracted. Then he said
abruptly, "It would be different."

Sylvia waited while he poked the fire, and she
noticed how his hand shook. When he began
again, he had tried to resume his quiet, unemo-
tional manner: —

"I have not the physique, the strength. I had
not the constitution. But I did not know. And
I tried."

There was a tragedy of failure in those few
words. His face worked, and he got up and
turned his back upon Sylvia, and walked slowly
the length of the room. It seemed to her that
she must cry out in her pain and pity, but she
clenched her hands and sat still.

"I had spent years of study upon it," he said,
coming back and sitting down once more; "I
had worked upon the scales, the trills, the exer-
cises, until my voice was as flexible, as even, as
smooth! — there was not a rough place in it.
They gave me the best masters here, and those
were very good. I had a little money of my own
left from my father, a very little. When I was
twenty-two, I had been studying six years; my
voice changed early. There was a great singer

who came here, and I was introduced to her, and she heard me sing. She took a fancy to me. When she went away, I went, too, in her opera company. There was a place for me, by chance. It made maman unhappy; she wished me to remain at home. Jacques was very angry; he called me hard names, but he does not appreciate these things. If I had made my name as a great singer, they would have been proud. I knew this, and so I went away, but I did not tell them; I could not bear to give my mother pain, and they did not know that I had gone until it was the next day."

These occasional quaint lapses in Jocelin's English only enhanced the ordinary precision of his phrases. Sylvia, listening to him, could not but wonder, now and then, where he had learned the language. His enunciation was utterly different from that of Jacques; for while, on the one hand, he had retained distinct traces of accent in his voice, and Jacques only betrayed his French origin at rare intervals by a misplacement of emphasis upon syllables, on the other hand he gave his words a roundness, an exactness, an almost Bostonian finish, which were entirely absent from the speech of his step-brother, who flattened his "a's" like a true Southerner.

There had been another long pause, during which the frankness with which Jocelin acknowledged his running away went far to justifying the act in Sylvia's mind.

"It was in Memphis that I sang. And it was
not as large an opera house as ours. There was
a fashionable audience, — very polite, — I only
heard one little hiss. But if there had been
more hisses, it would have been preferable. She
said to me after it was over, ' I was afraid of it.
They could not hear you, my friend; they missed
the fine work because of lack of power. It is an
exquisite voice, but we must make up our minds
to the fact that it is not meant for grand opera.'
She would have had me stay with her. She was
fond of me. But I loved my voice better than I
loved her. It stifled me to remain with her, and
I went away. I had dreamed, and dreamed, and
I had labored, building, polishing, finishing that
voice. I do not understand why I was born.
The failure of my voice was due to faults that
were not mine. It is unjust! The doctors said
to me, ' You must take care of yourself, Mr. Castaigne; it is an inherited delicacy of constitution.' I was angry when they told me that, and
I said, ' What do they mean?' And I bought
a medical book and read their jargon. I think
there was one word in it I could comprehend,
and that was 'ancestry.' And I thought of that
man there on the wall, whose nose I possess. ' I
was still away from home; but he is historical, so
I could get a book about him and his sons and
his sons' sons. Then I understood! They had
thrown me the rags of their flesh and the dregs

of their blood, these ancestors; they had sighed a last gasp of genius into my soul.   In the North, where I strayed for three years, I learned that these ideas were well known, were ordinary, but to me they were new.   When I can sing with art, and more than art, with something that even in my poor voice can hold and stir men's hearts, must I sit down and let that fellow at the opera house come out and sing Rigoletto's song, and bellow, and be heard and praised, — because he is not so well born as I, and his strength has not been sapped, and the root of his tree is not rotten and dead?   Is it any satisfaction to me to know that I sing it better than he does?"

There was a hopeless note ringing through his voice and his rapid words.   He had forgotten himself for the moment in his grief.

"I obtained positions in theatrical companies, sometimes in comic opera, to sing, sometimes only to act.   I despised it, but there was no hope, and I did not care.   I did many wicked things."   He had returned to his impassive tone. "I did many wicked things; I did not care.   I drank; I was very dissipated.   And all that was not good for my voice; it is weaker now than it used to be, and less elastic.   You tell me it is a beautiful voice now, mademoiselle, — but if you had heard it three years ago!   I was desperate, and I did not care.   And yet I can say this, " — he looked at Sylvia with wistful guilelessness, — "I have never harmed any one but myself."

Sylvia had been unpleasantly conscious, all along, of the singer who was fond of him, and whom he left because he did not love her as dearly as he loved his voice; and now she felt a sense of relief which inclined her to take, perhaps, a more lenient and humble-minded view of his excesses than was at all necessary under the circumstances.

Jocelin was not a liar; it was simply that, when he made a statement, the actions in his life which might have contradicted this statement went out from his mind as cleanly as if they had never been. Indeed, for the moment, they were to him as if they were not. He was entirely unconscious of falsehood in the matter. Moreover, it is perfectly possible that, even while keeping the singer in mind, Jocelin could still, irrespective of the facts of the affair, have made that magnanimous remark. There are so many ways of looking at a thing, you know. What is black on a dove may not show on a crow. This aspect of the case did not occur to Sylvia for two or three years.

Jocelin had no intention of deceiving Sylvia; on the contrary, he was showing her the self in him that he most believed in, and the simplicity of his confession, "I have been very dissipated," only added to his charm. It was such an unusual, such a childlike, statement. If he knew this, he did not, therefore, repress it. Jocelin was a queer mixture of naïveté and art. The point of division between where he had tried to produce an effect, and where he had produced an effect without trying, was difficult to distinguish. In his pleasures he showed great catholicity of taste, — at the present moment his soul asked for no higher bliss than to sit in this quiet, firelit room, and watch this spirit-like Puritan girl, and talk to her of his ideals and his disappointments. But it is equally true that, in the midst of revelry and feasting and wine, his soul turned face about and went joyously the way of all flesh. It is hard to say in which of these rôles his grace and charm of childlikeness proved the more effective and dangerous.

"No, I have never harmed any one but myself," he repeated shamelessly, and the radiance of candor suffused his liquid eyes.

"It is a great deal to be able to say that," murmured Sylvia.

She knew that she ought to initiate him into the ethical problem of his responsibility towards his own soul, but once more she said to herself, "The world is in a hurry, — let it go!"

Jocelin smiled a lovable, modest smile. He felt very modest, very humble, very repentant, as he confessed his sins to this unspotted, unsuspicious woman. He had sinned, but not yet often enough for remorse to have begun to bite through the pleasure of repentance.

"I have been in Philadelphia, New York, Boston, Washington, all the large cities of the North. I learned my English in the theatrical companies. Before that, I had known very little of Americans. Jacques went to the American University, but I went to a French school. Jacques and I were always different. In New York I got a place in a church, after a time, and I sang at one or two houses in the evenings. People liked my voice; they pay well for that sort of thing; I was beginning to 'take,' as they say in slang. But imagine, mademoiselle! I had not seen my home and my mother, and my little sister, for three years. I was racked with homesickness, that terrible sensation. The choir-master said ' Stay;' he was most anxious, but nothing would induce me to do so. I could not; it was an impossibilité. Figure to yourself, mademoiselle, the desire. I was miserable, and I returned home."

"And you mean that you were beginning to gain, to have some success, and you gave it all up?" said Sylvia.

"But consider that terrible homesickness!" said Jocelin; "I felt that I should die if I did not return. On the whole, I am not doing so badly here. It has taken a long while, but I have a pupil now, and I sing in some choirs. I earn a little money, and for the rest, — my life is already over. As for that, it never began, it only — how do you say? — baulked."

He smiled wistfully over his little joke, and, twisting around on the piano-stool, began to play again softly.

There were many evenings that winter when Sylvia talked to Jocelin, tried to rouse him, tried to reason with him, but to-night she could not do these things. His moral depression and inactivity were too like her own; they made her feel faint and ashamed, and she wanted to hide her face. Who was she, that she should deem herself worthy to show him the necessity for struggle and action? The words of rebuke and exhortation which the occasion demanded fell back in her throat and choked her. There was something very like fright in her eyes as she stared into the fire, for she had been twisted around into sitting in judgment upon her own soul, and, with all her introspection and self-reproach, this was something she had not done before.

The melody flickered and flushed with the fire-shadows, and there was silence for a while between the two quiet, flame-lighted figures, the Puritan and the Creole, who had come along their widely separated paths to the place where two roads meet, and now lay idle at the cross-ways. Back, back, along his road, along the track of his life, and the track of the lives that

had gone to the making and marring of his, far
back as you chose to listen, there came a sound
of laughter and revel, a clashing of swords, a
clinking of wine-cups, a rumble of oaths, and a
musical flow of words that were poems. And,
looking, you saw, behind 'and beyond on the road,
pale, drink-sodden, passionate faces, and slender
white fingers that trembled; and, backward still,
beauty, and pride of bearing, and gay-colored
garments. You saw debauch, and chivalry, and
brilliant wit, on that road. Genius and Love-of-
Pleasure came down all the length of it, sinning
together, now one, now the other pursuing, pol-
luting, polluted, and languid with passion. And
there at the cross-roads Jocelin lay. One leap
for him, and he came to the end of it quickly.
And there at the cross-roads lay Genius and
Love-of-Pleasure, pale, stupid, and sick of each
other; but the will to fling off and abandon the
one, the other, was gone.

Look now on the strait and narrow way
whence Sylvia came. Gray-garmented figures,
demure in their glances and staid in their gait,
pass onward. The murmurs of prayers are the
poems, the terrible exhortation of preachers is all
the sound of riot along this road. In the dead
of night, if you walked, you stumbled on kneeling figures that knelt the long night through,
immovable, wrestling in the spirit. Look onward and into the faces of those who travel

sedately this road. The faces of men are steeled
to contemplate the logic of justice and judgment
their intellect bids them accept as the end of
creation. The faces of mothers are thin and
drawn with the terror of bearing children des-
tined, perhaps, to go down headlong to destruc-
tion. And oh, the faces of children! Turn
away and weep! Caution, bewilderment, irresolution, totter along by the wayside.

Sylvia's people came this way. Down this
road comes Genius, too, sister to that other, a
brilliant, thinking creature with wings of iris.
Down this road comes Master Puritan What-is-
my-Duty, terrified, shrinking, loving the rainbow
Genius, — loving and loved in turn, — wistfully,
sadly, submissively. And between is the width
of the roadway, all too narrow for terror and in-
decision. Always the roadway lies between, and
Genius and What-is-my-Duty tremble along its
edges, eying each other, wasting thinner with
longing.

This is the road along which Sylvia, doubting
herself, staggered a little space before she lay
down at the cross-ways. And over her body,
standing one on each side, Genius and What-is-
my-Duty look at each other, so tired, so thin!
and the will to touch is gone, and the fear of
each other is gone, and they do not care.

Something of all this Jocelin felt and Sylvia
thought, in the quaint, dim room where the music

and the shadows mingled. Something of this, but only a dim, vague something, incomplete. And the one mind lapped itself in the pleasure of sitting still in a sympathetic and comprehending silence with a pure woman, and the other mind stiffened with terror at the recognition of its own sympathy with and comprehension of a psychical state which it saw to be the result of sin.

Madame opened her eyes and peered around sleepily. Sylvia glanced at the clock, and, finding the hands at a quarter past eleven, rose and said good-night, and thanked Jocelin for the evening. When she had gone, he went down to the courtyard and smoked the long-deferred cigarette.

An hour later Enid peeped cautiously into Sylvia's room, and, hearing a gentle "Don't be afraid! I'm awake," came in, lit the gas, and sat on the edge of the bed.

"Such a good time!" she said. "I wished for you. Some of the voices were good, and there was a full house. So many pretty women! I was introduced to a lot of men, all more or less uninteresting, rather vapid creatures, — chit-chatty, you know. But I think they felt I must be worth cultivating, as I was in Miss Campion's box."

She laughed with a quizzical, shamefaced look, and Sylvia laughed, too.

"But I quite enjoyed Mr. Dumarais. He has

gotten over expecting me to flirt or languish, and
he is really very good company. We spent two
of the intermissions promenading in the foyer,
and quarreling violently, first over the Lottery
Question, and then over the Italians again. He
is not on the Lottery side, not in the least; believes it's wrong and all that, but calmly says he
buys a ticket every month. It is absolutely in-
consistent, you know, and I tried to make him
see it, and he laughed and said, ' Ah, bah! '
You couldn't make him reason it out or connect
it with the general question. He only smiled
and looked amused and superior. There was no
making him dissatisfied; he didn't seem to have
any moral feeling in the matter at all. It was
like the unmoral fairy creatures who never did
wrong because right and wrong had not begun
to be differentiated for them. I can't understand
it. And, Sylvia dear, I wish you could have seen
Jeanne! She has all the pretty, trembling alter-
nation between assurance and timidity that goes
to make a success in what we call society. I
never recognized it so clearly before. She was
perfectly bewitching, and all the men, old and
young, were hovering round, beaming upon her.
Miss Campion said again and again, ' Isn't she
charming! ' and her step-brother was so proud
and pleased! There was a glamour about her,
and yet it was not in what she said; her conversation had no more thought in it than that of a

well-brought-up child; but it was so pretty, with
that childlike originality about it which appeals
to men as feminine. I am so glad that she is to
have a happy winter. As we came upstairs, Mr.
Jacques put his arm around her and kissed her,
and she threw her arms about his neck with a
kind of ecstasy and said, 'You were pleased,
Jacques, were n't you?' I — I — Dear little
thing! But she is n't the sort of woman that
will appeal to him, I 'm afraid. He is much
more intellectual than she, even if he is so pig-
headed. And did you have a nice evening? Did
he sing well?"

"Beautifully!" said Sylvia. "I do not believe your Rigoletto sang the song after the betrayal so well."

"Perhaps not," replied Enid. "Oh, my dear!
the funniest thing was the women's chorus, —
large, fat, aged creatures! Oh, so homely!
You should have heard Roma Campion's remarks
about them. She has not that regard for the
manners and customs of her native place which
seems to be inborn in most of the other people
we have met here. But I must not keep you
awake a minute longer. I am so glad you enjoyed your evening, too. Tell me about it to-
morrow. "

"He told me all about his life, poor man!"
whispered Sylvia. "It has been very sad."

"Well, dear, you must n't lie awake mourning

over it. If it is sad, I've no doubt he helped to make it so. There! I didn't mean to be unappreciative. He is a dear, thoughtful young man, and I like him, and I am really sorry for him. But you mustn't stay awake."

"Don't you think," faltered Sylvia, "that although you have the sorrows of humanity at heart, sometimes you are a little impatient of the sorrows of particular men?"

"Yes," answered Enid; "I do think so, but not of particular women."

She laughed as she said this, and, leaning over, kissed her friend.

"No, — I know," said Sylvia penitently; "and I, of all people, ought to be the last to accuse you of not caring for the individual, when I remember what you are constantly doing just for my sake."

"I shall say ' Ah, bah! ' as Monsieur Jacques does when he wishes to dismiss a subject," said Enid lightly. "And now good-night!"

Sylvia lay awake another hour.

"Because he is so like myself," she thought, "because he is tired and discouraged, I must try to help him. As far as I am concerned, my own illness and uselessness in the world need not prevent me from helping him to be useful, if I can. I cannot be anything for myself, but I must try to help him to be something. I can do that, — I can try to do that, for he has confided

in me. I must help him. I must. It does not
matter about myself; this is only pride, this
desire in me to be something. If I had been
meant to do anything in the world, I should have
tried long ago, just as he tried; he is better than
I. Because I have not made an effort, it shows
I could not. I wonder if I could really do it if I
— if — I wonder if Enid is right when she says I
could — if I would? She believes in the fragments I have done. It is all fragments. The
days go, and I never begin the blending of the
fragments. I wonder if I could! I want to, —
oh, I want to! Oh, I want to! Why? I wonder
if I could? I wonder if I should fail as he did,
if I tried, from lack of power? I think so. I
wonder, — oh, Enid, I would try, if I thought
you were right. I am so tired, — and so is he.
I 'll let myself alone. I 'll give myself up. I
must help him. I will! "

This thought was the beginning of the salvation of Sylvia.

BOOK II

JEANNE'S WINTER

" At length burst in the argent revelry,
  With plume, tiara, and all rich array,
  Numerous as shadows haunting fairily
  The brain, new-stuff'd in youth with triumphs gay
  Of old romance."

JOHN KEATS.

CHAPTER I

MATRIMONY SERIOUSLY CONSIDERED

CHRISTMAS came and went, mild and sunny. *Le Jour de l'An* passed by, and Jeanne's winter whirled merrily on towards Twelfth Night and the Carnival, and Jeanne whirled with it. Jacques had nothing to complain of; she was living up to all her social opportunities with a successfulness that left nothing to be desired; and, truth to tell, Jacques was very proud of her. He used to stand aside with Enid and watch the little sister with paternal satisfaction and amusement as she danced by, looking over her shoulder to nod and smile. That little nod and smile were always ready when he chose to look her way. "Are you pleased? Do you approve?" her eyes said to him twenty times in an evening, and sometimes he smiled back "Yes," and sometimes he was so busy talking to Enid that he stared straight through the question in the eyes, and only knew, a moment later, that it was Jeanne who had passed by and looked at him. When she pretended to pout and be cross with him, saying, perhaps: —

"But, Jacques, you did not dance with me a single time last evening!" —

He would answer, "Why should I? It is only the girls who do not have many partners who need to be looked after by their brothers. I should have had half a dozen young fellows about my ears last night if I had tried to monopolize you."

And she would laugh and blush, not more than half appeased, but unwilling to say so, since Jacques always knew best.

"There is no show for any of the rest of us when Dumarais is around," one of the young men said laughingly once. He said it with the best intentions, under the impression that he was giving pleasure to Jacques; but it put Jacques absurdly out of temper, and he said "Ah, bah!" and scowled, and told the innocent young man not to be an idiot.

Jacques' business arrangements were still unsettled. His firm, when apprised of his intention to withdraw from them, came forward handsomely, and made offers which Curtis Baird insisted that he should consider. So January was passing, and Jacques was debating over two offers instead of one, and certain of increasing his income, no matter which one he should decide to accept. Six months ago, a hint that he might hope for success, if he cared to lay siege to the heart of his pretty step-sister, would not have troubled him in the least; he would have dismissed it with his usual melancholy "I cannot afford to marry." Nay, more than this, six months ago such a hint would have pleased and flattered him. What had happened to him that to-day he should fall into a rage with the well-meaning suggester of such a possibility? To-day, when the financial obstacles to his marriage were removed!

"It's a shame to set on foot a report like that!" he blustered within himself, thinking the matter over, for it tormented him. "It's a shame! It does not give a girl half a chance to do well for herself. No fellow is going to pay serious attentions to her, if he thinks she's already as good as engaged to another man."

Did you wish her to fall in love with some one else, then, Jacques? Was it that you considered yourself less desirable as a *parti* than the numerous impecunious young clerks, with seventy-five dollars a month and no prospects, who fluttered foolishly about your step-sister? Were you convinced that some middle-aged club-man would be more desirable as a husband than you? Didn't you want to marry her, Jacques?

"It would spoil all her fun, if I let such a rumor get about," he reasoned; "it isn't fair to her. She has never seen anything of the world. She doesn't know her own mind. I'll see if I can't arrange to send her North next summer, and give her a taste of something different."

He could not dismiss the subject from his mind; it ran along as an undercurrent beneath all his decisions and debatings concerning his business arrangements.

"Hang it all!" he swore at his pertinacious and offending self-consciousness. "A man has n't got to start in and get married just the very minute he 's able to. If I had n't these offers, I could n't marry, and there would be an end to it. I don't see why the case should be any different now, or the necessity any more urgent."

Then he would experience a revulsion of sentiment, and would call himself a conceited ape for presuming to think that she cared for him in such a way. Was n't he the same as a brother to her? Had n't they lived together all their lives? Did n't he really stand to her in the place of a father? She loved him, but did n't he love her? She was no fonder of him than he was of her. And then, perhaps, across a crowded room he would meet the inquiry in her loving brown eyes, and his impatience and irritation would vanish, leaving a strange heartache in their stead, for indeed he was very fond of this little sister.

"Of course, if I were in love with any one else," he argued, "it would be different, entirely different. But I 'm not, — I 'm not!"

He assured himself of this fact fretfully. "I 'd like to see anybody accuse me of being in love with any one else!"

And at this juncture he usually excused himself from Enid and went in search of Jeanne, and put his name down for a dance, or took her off to get a glass of punch.

But there were other times when, talking with Enid, he forgot to watch uneasily for Jeanne's glance; forgot to declare that he was in love with no one else; forgot everything, except that this handsome woman with the clear voice was the most entertaining and appreciative comrade he had ever had. He began to compare her with the other women of his acquaintance, and decidedly to the detriment of those other women. He began to forget to apologize for talking to her as if she were a man. He began to turn with relief from chatter about Miss This and Mr. That, the details of the newest engagement or the latest ball, and the vapid flippancies that pass for wit, to this serious-minded woman's conversation about life.

For she was serious-minded, — there was no denying it; but so was Jacques. Society seldom guessed it, because there was not a more ridiculous, noisy, nonsensical creature than he when he chose to be; and hitherto this sort of buffoonery, varied with sentimental tête-à-têtes and flirtations, had been all that his social world had demanded of him; so he kept the steady worth of himself for business, flinging the froth of his cleverness contemptuously to womankind. And yet, with true French contradictoriness, there was no one more gentle, more chivalrous to women than Jacques. It is to be doubted whether he would have been attracted towards Enid, if he had not lived in the house with her; for he had the conservative Southern man's prejudice against modern women and higher education, and always went out of his way to avoid women with views. Fortunately, or unfortunately (who shall decide which?), he was not permitted to avoid Enid; he was, compelled to see her and talk with her day after day. And Enid was a person who wore well. He did not always quarrel with her; oftener than not he agreed with her, and delighted in following out her line of thought, saying: —

"Why, of course, of course, I believe that. Always have."

The kind of socialistic thought he had gained from Hugo she modernized and developed for him; and when he at last learned that she taught this sort of thing and lectured about it, instead of being shocked and disgusted, as he ought in all consistency to have been, he was radiant with enthusiasm and respect.

Then, too, the womanly side of Enid came out in her care of Sylvia. The little sacrifices she made, which were really no sacrifices at all, in staying at home when Sylvia was ill or tired, appealed to him. Jacques admired Sylvia, as

who did not? And, in common with the rest of
humanity, he treated her as something a little
finer than mortal clay; but she did not attract
him, and, moreover, Jocelin had assumed the
right to attend to her small wants. As has been
said, Jacques was a person of prejudices, and the
people whom Jocelin singled out as objects of
favor were likely to lose interest for his step-
brother.

It was a pleasure, after a hard day spent in
trying to outdo one's fellow-creatures on the
Cotton Exchange, to return home and relax one's
mind by a discussion of the brotherhood of man.
Men — the kind of commonplace, half-educated,
eager-for-a-dollar young men he knew — did not
talk of things like this. Theories and theorizing
were not customary among them; club gossip,
newspaper politics, were the things they, the
business men, talked about.

Yes, Enid wore well. And, in addition, it
must not be forgotten that she was a handsome
woman.

Meanwhile, what was Enid making of Jacques'
evident and growing enjoyment of her society?
Did she understand what it meant? It is useless
to attribute to Enid, at twenty-eight, that obtuse-
ness towards admirers, that unconsciousness of
being loved, with which certain novels, notably
those romantic ones translated from the German,
insist upon slandering their young and sentimen-

tal heroines. Enid is too old to come in gracefully under this canon of romantic fiction. Besides, Enid had had too little of this kind of attention in her life, and was too much of a woman
not to have felt mortified at not attracting it,
to be oblivious of its presence now. It flattered
her not to have him grow to take an interest in
her because of Miss Campion's patronage, but
because of her own personality. At the same
time, she never meant to give him pain; she did
not believe the feeling would go deep enough
for pain. Their attitude towards each other was
devoid of all sentimentality; they were merely
good comrades; and she took care to give him
such an insight into her life, its claims, its activi-
ties, its ideals, as should make him clearly understand the minimum of attention she could afford
to bestow upon him.

Of the tumult of uncertainty which was growing up in his mind — above all, of his feeling
about Jeanne, — she had not the slightest inkling.
How could she have? This was what he was
most assiduous in concealing. She saw him jest
with the little sister, tease her, put his arm
around her; she saw him smile at her in the dance
with brotherly interest, and she became more
and more convinced that Jeanne's type was not
the type of woman he needed for a wife; and she
became more and more sorry for Jeanne, but
glad that he did not guess Jeanne's feelings.

The last thing that he wished to confess, at present, was that he guessed Jeanne's feelings.

"No, I'm not in love with any one else," quoth Jacques; "and besides, if I were, it wouldn't be any use: she wouldn't have me; she's too much engrossed in other affairs to have time for matrimony. Poor little girl! If I were to fall in love with somebody else, what a brute I'd be! But if I were in love with somebody else, would it be right to marry — which? You are a fool, Jacques, a conceited fool! Does she ever show the slightest jealousy towards your attentions to — other women? See her now, dancing with that good-looking young fellow! Her heart is as light as her little French heels. Mon Dieu! why does the child look at me like that?"

CHAPTER II

NOT the least enjoyable of the many pleasant events of Jeanne's winter were the days spent in Miss Campion's old-fashioned Southern house in the American quarter, — a low house, classic with many pillars; a roomy structure, spread prodigally over the ground. and set in the midst of a garden.

Here Miss Campion abode grudgingly for as much as seven months of the year, with her father, her grandmother, two younger brothers, and a staff of colored retainers. Her morning-room opened on two sides, and through three French windows, upon the wide-roofed gallery, and through one door into the great hall, which was also sitting-room and library. In this morning-room she read and embroidered and fretted, and again took heart of grace; she planned her gowns and her little dinners, than which were none in New Orleans more charming; she rejected her lovers, fascinated her victims, and dominated her little world. When she would she arose and went to Europe, and that meant Paris, and that meant shops. When she could, she lingered in New York, inventing excuses — the weather, the horse-show, the opening night of the Wagner opera — for staying away from the picturesque house with the fluted and fawn-colored columns, half hidden by the palm shrubs, the sweet olive and jessamine bushes, that grew in the garden, and half smothered by rose-vines along the southwestern exposure, which was the morning-room corner.

But grandmamma, a charming and stately old lady with white hair à la Pompadour, loved New Orleans, and papa had a bank there, and a plantation down the river; so, some time before the first snowstorm arrived in the North, Miss Campion began to loiter unwillingly homeward.

It was strange, this hatred of the South and all things Southern, in one who was born and bred a Southerner. The companions of her girlhood were convinced that no place in the universe was quite as gay, as hospitable, as tasteful, as New Orleans; that no women were quite as beautiful and bewitching as the Southern women, and no men quite as gallant, as entertaining, as desirable, as the Southern men. But this was not Miss Campion's conviction.

The typical, the ordinary New Orleans girl serenely moves upon her way, convinced that, if New York women are richer and more tailor-made, she has more French *chic* and charm; and, if Bostonians are better educated, she has more intuitive intelligence and wit. She knows all these things because she has read them in books, or else somebody has told her so, — somebody who wanted to be agreeable. The term "Southern girl," used in Northern society, suggests some one who is pretty, *piquante*, and altogether "good fun." It is a signal for the society men to prick up their ears and look interested. Undoubtedly one is excusable for feeling complacent under such circumstances. That is, if complacency is ever excusable.

Miss Campion scorned the self-satisfaction, the naïve rejoicing in its own charms, which her native city openly displayed. She tried to instill this haughty discontent into her little sisters, but without success; they were proving themselves two as placid, self-satisfied, provincial little creatures as ever had been born.

Miss Campion went forth into the great world of great wealth and great alliances and great scandals, — went forth and reigned, saying: "This is power! This is life!" And by and by came home reluctantly to the little world of little wealth and little alliances and little scandals, — came home, and failed to see that here was simply a distinction without a difference. She dominated her little world, and when she looked upon it, it smiled and prostrated itself obsequiously, and behaved with a servility that would have made any right-minded person scornful. And when she looked away, it showed its teeth and spit venom and malice-of-envy.

And of course opinions differed as to whose fault all this might be.

She watched the complacent friends of her girlhood drift away into matrimony, maternity, occasionally into divorce. She watched other girls come on the social stage, and drift away in their turn, and she held her own in the presence of younger smiles and fresher faces. And she took satisfaction in her triumph. But as the years passed, the eternity of the thing began to pall upon her; it grew monotonous, this ever-repeated conquest. What to do next? At thirty she could not see anything that was worth doing; and yet, when she looked in her mirror, she said: "I must do something soon! Why does it all bore me so?"

To a woman of her education and standard, marriage was the only something to be done at the present crisis. Her world had waited on this event for ten years, and she had teased her world, and coquetted with it, and laughed at it, and said: "I will whomsoever I will, when I will. But as yet I will not!" And this was a part of her triumph. But of late it had ceased to be a triumph; it had become an annoyance.

"Why do you stand expectant?" she fumed; "you bore me! Have done! I will not!"

And still, in her heart of hearts, she knew that she would. The thing was expected of her. She must!

She thought of half a dozen men she might have if she would, and she wanted none of them. And about this time Enid and Sylvia came into her life; Enid and Sylvia, untroubled by lack of suitors, indifferent to matrimony, — women as old as herself, or nearly so, ten times more learned, and withal so childlike, so direct and simple. She turned to them with a hope of salvation. Might not she become like them? Might not she do as they were doing? Was not this one way of escape? — one way of cheating her world? That was the thing she wanted to do more than all, if she dared, — cheat this impudent world that presumed to dictate and say "You must!"

She took more comfort in her friendship with these two women than she had ever before taken in the society of her own sex. Enid and Sylvia kept their sarcasms for generalizations instead of for individuals; they made no personal thrusts which she must be on her guard to parry; they did not seek to wound her by pretending to compliment. Their genuine liking, and frankness of friendship, stirred in her heart a tenderness that affected her like a grief; and there were nights when she sobbed herself to sleep with tears as passionate and pathetic as those of a child who

bears a slight in silence stubbornly, and responds
to unlooked-for sympathy with a storm of weeping.　And she a woman of thirty!

Her softened mood made her dangerously susceptible to the persistent wooing of Curtis Baird,
if she had but known it.

Her new friends spent long days with her.
She took them to drive; she learned their ways,
their pursuits, their enthusiasms, with as much
care and slow reflection as she would have be-
stowed upon a book.　Often Jeanne made one of
the party, — Jeanne, who seemed to Miss Campion
a picture of her own gay, careless youth, ideal-
ized, with the ambition left out.　She was very
tender to Jeanne; she petted her; she made
much of her.　Curtis Baird liked to sit beside
Miss Campion and note the gentle, preoccupied
smile which came into her face at sight of the
happy little French girl.　There were several
people watching Jeanne that winter.　And
Jeanne repaid Miss Campion's kindness by a
girlish adoration and no criticism.

The younger Campion girls, away at school,
were growing up cold, self-sufficient little mortals, small comfort to their elder sister.

"I believe Roma is considering this Mr. Baird
rather seriously," said Madame Campion to her
son.　She and her grand-daughter never told
each other their *affaires de cœur.*

"A fine fellow!" said Mr. Campion, who

loved Roma dearly, but was at times perplexed by her caprices.

And Roma kept her own counsel in the matter, and would not acknowledge to herself, even for a moment, that she meant to accept him. And yet, when the time came, she did.

Meanwhile she cultivated her new friends, and strove in every way to make them enjoy the social atmosphere in which she moved, watching them curiously to see if they really did enjoy it.

"And you never expect to marry?" she said once in her direct, attentive way.

Jeanne, Enid, and Sylvia were sitting in the pretty morning-room, talking, in a more or less desultory fashion, about the future of woman. Enid, to whom this question was addressed, laughed, it was put with such weight and solemnity.

"I wouldn't go so far as to take a solemn oath on the subject," she replied; "I should be afraid, if I did, I might find that I wanted to some day. Of course, if it ever seemed the right thing to do, I should do it, but I certainly don't want to now. I haven't time; I have too many other things to do, — too many other things I would rather do."

"Really!" said Miss Campion. This "really" was such an attractive word when she said it! She added, with a certain impatience: "I have been educated with the idea that it showed stupidity to be an old maid. My little sisters are already beginning to regard me as a grievance ; it is funny to see the superior airs they give themselves when I offer them my opinion. I am afraid I should feel as if I had n't managed my life cleverly, if I did not marry. I should feel ashamed of myself. Absurd, is n't it, to make such a confession as that? It is refreshing to get your point of view."

"I have been sorry for married women oftener than for old maids," said Enid curtly.

Jeanne's eyes opened inquiringly. "You mean they discover they do not love each other?" she asked. "But then, that is not the general rule."

"My dear little Jeanne, there are many reasons why people should not marry each other," said Enid.

There were times when Jeanne's innocence seemed to her a criminal thing, and she said to herself with a kind of rage : —

"In a year, perhaps less, they will let this guileless, ignorant, helpless creature marry. They will somehow imagine they have rendered a service to humanity by keeping her as ignorant of life, and as unprepared for it, as if she were still a babe in arms."

With the child sitting beside her, she dared not rail aloud at this ignorance, but it annoyed her.

"Perhaps even you might do better than marry,

Jeanne. You might cultivate that musical talent of yours, you lazy little sprite."

"Oh, but I don't think so!" laughed Jeanne; "I would rather think Miss Campion's way. I told Jacques what you said about my music that time, and he laughed at me, and said one musician was all we could afford in the family, for they were expensive luxuries."

She flushed when she had said it, realizing that she had been rather too outspoken about her family affairs, and Miss Campion patted her cheek and said caressingly : —

"If I had a daughter, Jeanne, I should wish her to be just like you."

Miss Campion had the wise and weary woman's sentimental liking for *l'ingénue*. She would n't have been one herself, — no, not for worlds! but she liked to think she regretted her own initiation into the realities of life.

"And so you want this child to give herself seriously to music?" she said, turning to Enid. "Do you think she would be any happier?"

It was Sylvia who answered the question, saying : —

"No, I do not think she would be, after all. Some of us don't do a thing because we want to be happy, at least consciously we don't; but some of us seem to have to do the happy things, — we are meant to, — and I believe Jeanne was meant to."

It was not usual for Sylvia to take part in the conversation; she liked best to be silent. This readiness to reply always meant gain in health.

"Yes," assented Enid, "I really do think so, too, but I can't resist trying to make Jeanne a bit discontented with herself. Very naughty of me, is n't it, Jeanne?"

"Do you also belong to committees, and give lectures when you are well, as this busy woman does?" asked Roma of Sylvia.

She had not asked about Sylvia's life before; it had impressed her as an invalid life, — a life that leaned upon Enid's stronger vitality and followed Enid's lead.

"Sylvia is going to be the literary medium for my efforts," said Enid. "Yes, I will tell. You need not look at me and shake your head. We are a partnership, Sylvia and I. I am the man about town, the planner, the promulgator. Sylvia sits in the counting-room and cashes the checks, and she is to keep the record of events, and lay the affairs of the firm before the public in good literary form. You really don't know anything about Sylvia. I 'm the showy person, but Sylvia takes all my little theories and turns them inside-out before my eyes, and clothes them in metaphor and metre."

"You write, then?" said Miss Campion eagerly.

"No!" said Sylvia, gazing imploringly at her communicative friend.

"She does!" cried Enid. "She has written ever since she could hold a slate-pencil."

Enid was in a jubilant frame of mind, and her joy bubbled out in these reckless revealings of Sylvia's desires.

Sylvia was better. The change was a subtle one, but Enid, who knew her well, could be sure of it. It could not be called a physical improvement as yet, for the headaches and the weariness were at times intense; but if she lay awake at night, the effects, for some reason, were not so injurious the next day. Enid knew that some interest other than Sylvia's self was at work in Sylvia's mind. What that interest was she did not yet know, but she could see that Jocelin had something to do with it.

Another symptom of improvement was that Sylvia had scribbled more than once of late; Enid had caught her at it. When the poor, self-torturing, self-distrustful mind could get far enough away from itself to act, this was always its first action. There was a pile of scraps of paper in Sylvia's desk at home, — bits of poems, some finished, some ending at the middle of the first stanza, as if frightened at their own temerity and discouraged with themselves; bits of disconnected thought in prose; beginnings of stories, the same story begun a dozen different ways and carried to

a dozen different lengths of incompleteness. Now
the thought that stopped the vacillating pen was,
"Have I a right, with my feeble constitution, to
tax my strength by doing this thing which makes
my head ache?" And, in trying to decide, the
headache would increase. Another time she
would question, "If I had the gift, would I not
write in spite of myself?" And she never seemed
to see how hard she was trying to write in spite
of herself. Again perhaps she would think, "If
it were written this other way, would it not be
better?" and she would write and re-write, growing more uncertain of herself and of her work
each moment, until she was positively incapable
of finishing what she had begun.

And then would follow days of darkness, in
which she resolutely withheld herself from writing,
turned from it with terror, wrestled in the night
with those sweet and terrible imaginings which
came to torture, to tempt her to begin again.

Sylvia's great-grandfather, it was said, wrote
a play in his youth, and went through life with
the stern belief that he was to enter into hell-fire
in the end. They said he had a beautiful face,
and eyes like Sylvia's. And he reared his one
son for the ministry, but the gift of the father
descended to the son, and the minister's sermons
were a snare to his mind, and the beauty of his
prayers was to him as the flesh-pots of Egypt;
he felt that he delighted in them more than he

delighted in his God, — which is not to be wondered at when one considers what kind of a God it was, — and so he went out of his mind, and people called him "the mad preacher."

And Sylvia's mother was a pious, pretty little girl, who married a well-balanced, prosperous man, and gave him a son like himself, but more brilliant. Three years after the birth of the boy, Sylvia came and the mother died.

Even a little improvement in her friend set Enid's heart singing for joy, and made her almost reckless.

"Some day," she said, "when we both know more about it and have lived in it, Sylvia is going to write the new novel of social regeneration. She can't do it yet, because we don't know enough; it has n't grown into us enough for us to make it real, but the life we get by my working she is going to hold fast in a book and send out to convert mankind."

Enid said this half laughing, with a kind of mockery at her own and Sylvia's powers, but there was a reality in it that surmounted the fun. This thing was a conviction with her, and all these women knew it.

"Sylvia, may I tell?" she whispered; "you know you said you would tell yourself some time, and it ought to be soon."

Then, without waiting for permission, she said with another laugh: —

"While Sylvia is working up her style to the proper pitch for the great undertaking, she does other things." Enid did not tell of all those sad, unfinished scraps of thought. "She does other things, and " —

"And," interrupted Sylvia, reaching out to take Jeanne's hand, and speaking slowly, softly, as was her wont, "if this is to be told, as this naughty person insists, I shall tell it myself. Listen, Jeanne. I made a little verse the other night in bed, and I want you to put it to music, and then I want Monsieur Jocelin to teach you how to write it down. I want him to do it. I think, Jeanne dear, he gets tired and sorrowful sometimes, and, if you were to ask him to teach you, it would please him; we all of us feel better when we keep ourselves busy, you know."

She glanced involuntarily at Enid and blushed, as if acknowledging that she had been in the wrong in her own idleness.

"But you are to write it, you know, Jeanne; he is to teach you, not to do it for you."

Jeanne looked astonished and said nothing.

"And now let us hear this verse," said Miss Campion.

So Sylvia gave it: —

> " The young Spring came to the world
>   And found me,
>   And put her arm around me ;
>   And close, like rose-petals curled
>   Up under a sheath still furled,

My heart at the heart of the young Spring's heart
Beat its music out; and the world
Crowned me."

Enid's eyes were shining and full of tears, and she went over and put her arms around Sylvia.

"She never did such a thing before!" she cried eagerly. "She never would say any of her things to any one before, no matter how much they begged."

And Sylvia smiled at her, with only a shadow of fear in the dark eyes, and said: —

"But if Monsieur Jocelin is to occupy himself in teaching her how to do it, of course I would have to tell about it."

They all had some of the pretty, flattering speeches to make concerning it, which one makes to one's amateur literary friends, and after a while Jeanne slipped away, carrying with her the lines, which Enid wrote on the back of an envelope, hurriedly, at Sylvia's dictation.

Then the talk drifted to model tenements and absentee landlordism, and such serious matters, as it had a habit of doing when Jeanne was not by. And Roma was shocked and indignant to find herself called an absentee landlord, and tried to defend her position, without knowing why she was called on to defend it, and also without any desire to change her comfortable habits of life. But now and then they stopped their chatter for a moment to listen to the soft, tentative notes of the piano across the hall, and the low humming of Jeanne's voice as she experimented with Sylvia's poem.

Then they would return to the discussion.

"You say you are bored; you have nothing to do; you cannot be interested in people just because they are people," said Enid to Roma; "but only try it! Do things without being interested, and perhaps the interest will grow."

The dead-weight of boredom which had settled down upon this woman seemed a hopeless thing to lift. Enid felt the inefficiency of her own tugs at the burden, and recognized that she was inefficient chiefly because she herself had not yet found out what it meant to be bored.

"They are interested. They care for life; they are not ennuyées," thought Miss Campion. "I will go to Boston next autumn. I will try to find out what the interest is. Anyway, I need not marry if I do not wish to. Yes, I will study the things they are doing; it will at least be something new. I will visit them in their model tenement in the slums."

But within ten days she had engaged herself to Curtis Baird.

CHAPTER III

THE CARNIVAL

In February, when Winter is clasping the North in his tightest and whitest and longest and last embrace, the best days of the year come down to dwell in New Orleans, the fair-weather days of the short Southern spring. They are a kind of Indian summer put the wrong way round of the calendar. Even the Southerners enjoy them, for "there is sure to be a cold snap in March, you know."

The dew-fresh February air has a taste with a tang to it, and is without the languor and the thick, sultry prophecies of April. The sunshine is just struggling out of its winter pallor; the city is full of people, who stare and smile curiously, and try to get snapshots at courtyards and praline-venders. The shop windows are gay with French organdies, with bright-colored silks and gauzes. Newspaper offices, public buildings, even commercial houses, put forth a strange, foreign-looking flag, consisting of three diagonal stripes, purple, yellow, and green, with a large crown in the middle on the yellow stripe. This is the

royal flag of the King of the Carnival. The news-
papers are full of his coming; cablegrams appear
in the foreign dispatches announcing the arrival
of the Royal Fleet at Suez, Tamatave, Colombo,
and other parts equally romantic and remote.
Proclamations are published, signed "Bathurst,
Lord Chamberlain," commanding all loving and
loyal subjects to make ready with rejoicing for
the coming of his Majesty Rex, — King Rex,
as the children call him. Mardi Gras is coming,
Mardi Gras is coming! The world, the weather,
and the people are all one laugh for joy.

Early in January, the pompous and magnilo-
quent invitations to the balls begin to be distrib-
uted by polite but secretive-looking messengers,
who carry lists of names, and are careful to make
sure they have come to the right house. And
later, through the post, the tiny, mysterious
dance-cards begin to arrive, the biddings to the
favored ones who are elected to dance the first,
or the third, or the second, or the fourth dance
with such and such a masquer at such and such
a ball.

For ten days before the great day, the Mardi
Gras, the fat day of rejoicing, the carnival rages.
All galleries overhanging the street must be
propped, by order of the law. Rex is careful for
the safety of his loving and loyal subjects, and
the holiday crowd twists in and out good-naturedly among the rough timbers and temporary

pillars. The king must pass the City Hall, and opposite, in the gay green square with its quaintly whitewashed tree-trunks, rows of rough wooden seats are set up, one above the other, circus-fashion.

The first balls of the carnival — those which have no preliminary street pageant — open with a series of tableaux. After these, crowded close upon one another, come four processions and three balls, all taking place between Monday morning and — properly speaking — Wednesday morning.

When this rich and varied programme was unfolded to Enid and Sylvia, they gasped and cried out: —

"We never can go through all that!"

"You can't, anyway!" said Enid decisively.

"Ah, don't you be a dragon, now!" said Jacques. "I would n't let her bully me, Miss Sylvia. Of course you can do it. Nobody gets tired in carnival week till it's all over. You must n't miss it. You won't see anything like it anywhere else. It's a magnificent sight and a unique one. Besides, everybody says this will be the most gorgeous carnival we 've had yet. You owe it to yourself not to miss it, after coming all this way."

"Yes, Miss Bennett," drawled Baird; "when Dumarais can go so far as to abandon his customary modesty and reserve concerning the attri-

butes of his native town, and indulge in enco-
miums of this extreme character, you may trust
me there is something in it."

Everybody laughed, Jacques loudest of all.
Curtis Baird had found this outspoken self-ap-
preciation one of the charms of the Southern
people.

"They are as pleased as a parcel of children
when you praise them," he reflected often, smiling to himself. "They perk and prink themselves, and ask strangers to compliment them on
their climate, their hospitality, and their pretty
girls, with as much ingenuousness as a baby of
six who invites her friends to admire her new
silk stockings. It is delightful! I never saw a
people, confessedly a society people, so entirely
free from ennui. Here they are, throwing themselves into this preposterous carnival make-believe
with the abandon of children at a dancing-school
festival. You wouldn't find a Northern city
capable of tossing dignity to the winds, and kick-
ing up its civic and social heels in this jolly
fashion. It takes imagination to do this sort of
thing, and that's what this people has as a people. It is the Southern temperament, I suppose."

And Mr. Curtis Baird, with human contradictoriness, had proceeded to single out for special
adoration that Southern woman, of all others,
least Southern in speech and tendencies, least
imaginative and volatile in temperament, and,

what was more important under the circumstances, least satisfied with her own city and her own people. It amused him to hear her rail, and he drew her on to say sharp things about New Orleans, its complacency and narrowness. He ought to have been troubled concerning the incompatibility of making New Orleans his home and this scornful, self-willed lady his wife, but he was n't. He had never had to choose which of two good things he would have; he had always taken both, and he expected to take both in this case. He knew, of course, that Roma had a right to know what her future life promised to be, before she accepted him, and he intended to wait till his business arrangements were formally announced before offering himself to her, but, somehow, he did n't. And when Roma accepted him, on the Sunday before Mardi Gras, she did not know that the dinner he was to give, and which she had helped him to plan, was given in order to announce, to those few most likely to be interested, that he and Jacques Dumarais were going into partnership.

He felt a little troubled when he went away from her Sunday night, — only a little, however, for he had heard women rail before, and had never attached much importance to their vehement expressions of like and dislike. Moreover, he consoled himself by telling her jokingly the next day that after Mardi Gras she might want

to break her engagement, and she replied, also
laughing, that in that case they would not announce it till after the crisis.

If Baird had been more of a business man, he
would have realized the importance of the two
steps he was taking, but it did not occur to him
that his arrangement with Jacques could in any
way hamper his movements. He never had been
hampered, and he expected to take his wife away
and keep her away as long as she liked. So
what few qualms he had, through leaving her so
long in ignorance of his plans, were easily stifled.

He did not find out for some time how angry
she was, and how seriously she did debate breaking that engagement. But she was proud; she
was ashamed to betray to him how little she really
loved him,—although he was quite aware that
she had accepted him chiefly from bewilderment.
Finally, as the case was with him, so it was with
her; the exigencies of the situation had very little
meaning for her, and in addition she fell into
that fatal error of believing that if, after her
marriage, she found they really must live in New
Orleans, she should be able to persuade him to
dissolve the partnership. For of one thing she
was fully convinced, — that, whatever her own
feelings might be towards him, he loved her.

So she let the matter drift, and made her prep-
arations for her wedding. And he, his little
panic abated, felt more sure of her than he ought

to have felt, and made many promises about going to Europe, and spending winters in New York, promises which Jacques, armed with the rectitude of business responsibility, and innocent of any strain in Baird's marital relations, compelled him, later, to break. In the end, it was hard to tell whether he or his wife had been most at fault. If she had chosen to break with him after the dinner, she might have done so, but she always said : —

"How could I with any self-respect? "

This dinner added one more festivity to the burden which their hospitable friends insisted upon imposing on the two Northern women; and Sylvia, longing to show her gratitude for the kindness, tried to insist, with the irresolution and lack of judgment of an invalid, that she should be allowed to see everything. But the dinner proved to be the last straw for Enid, and she took the importunate and obtuse Jacques into a corner and laid down the law to him vigorously.

"She can't do it, and I don't intend she shall. You don't know anything about what she can stand and what she can't. You are a great, strong, normal man; you're so unconscionably healthy that you're not fit to judge for people who are delicate, and I won't have you exciting her and making her fret."

"Yes 'm," said Jacques meekly.

"She is doing very well ; she sleeps better,

and her appetite is pretty good, and her head does n't bother her more than half the time. And I 'm not going to have her break down and lose the little she's gained, not for all the Mardi Gras in Christendom."

· "Yes 'm," said Jacques.

"I 'm going to everything," — Jacques' face brightened, — "and you must n't think we do not appreciate your kindness in getting all these invitations for us, — I know it must be you. But she is not going to everything."

Here Jacques' ridiculous exaggeration of meekness was too much for Enid, and she laughed.

"And — and — you may decide which ones you want her to see most, and we 'll try to arrange it."

So it was finally settled that Sylvia should go to the Atlanteans' Ball, should see the processions, and should have Curtis Baird's dinner, and a peep at Comus.

"I don't see why you insist on our going to the Atlanteans'," Enid objected, "when you say you have to go out of town that day, and won't be able to take us there."

"That is only another instance of my self-sacrificing disposition," explained Jacques. "You will learn to appreciate me after a while. This is a new society, and I hear it is very fine; and besides, you all have dance-cards for that ball."

"We have for most of the others, too," said

Enid. "I really think it is very queer that, although you have never had to go off on business before, you should be obliged to go on that day of all others. Why can't you postpone it?"

"Impossible!" said Jacques; and then, as if meditating ways and means in his mind, "Perhaps I shall be able to get back by the night train, and I'll hurry around in time to bring you home."

Jeanne gave a delightful chuckle, and hugged him and said: —

"Please, Miss Enid, you must go to this one; you will be sorry if you don't!"

And gradually Enid began to observe that most of the young men she met had engagements out of town or were going to stag dinners on one or other of the mysterious nights, and they all said: —

"You know they poke us off upstairs till after the masquers have had their fun, so what's the good of going early?"

And, finding that no one else asked questions, Enid and Sylvia ceased asking them, also.

Jacques was angelic in smoothing the way for Sylvia. He fully retracted his former insistent statements with unblushing ardor.

"After all, Miss Sylvia, I wouldn't try to go to Momus, if I were you; of course it's one of the prettiest, but if you go to the Atlanteans' you will get a good idea of all those early balls.

Keep your strength for the dinner. Baird is setting great store by that dinner, and he's such a good fellow it would be a pity to disappoint him."

In his own room Jacques said to himself: "Wasn't she just ready to take my head off, though? Awfully handsome. Gee! but doesn't she love that girl, — yes!"

Something curiously like tenderness came into his bright gray eyes as he thought about Enid's devotion to her friend.

Jocelin escorted them to the Atlanteans' Ball.

Jocelin came in "very handy" about this time, for he belonged to no association, had no stag dinners to attend, and no urgent business engagements in the country. Perhaps he would have liked to have, for he was more than ordinarily pessimistic and prone to take a hopeless view of his life.

"If I could get him to promise to keep himself straight, and to take care of his voice, he would keep his promise," thought Sylvia.

Jocelin was so gentle, so impressionable, so easily led, and withal so humble! A promise, he said, was a sacred thing. He had never broken a promise, but he did not feel that he could enter lightly into compacts; he had too deep a knowledge of his own nature; he had a dread of making promises, lest he should break them. All this he said in the abstract, and with-

out reference to any special promise; for when
Sylvia tried to particularize, to draw him into
a compact, there was no one more obtuse, more
evasive, more eel-like in wriggling away from
definite agreement, than Jocelin.

His dislike to committing himself made Sylvia
respect him, because she, also, had this same
terror of promising to do a thing. But it made
her misjudge him, too; for she drew her conclu-
sions from knowledge of her own heart, not Jocelin's. He took all the pity she chose to give
him, but as for living differently, — that was
another matter.

A gentle and interesting melancholy pervaded
his manner during those carnival days. He
walked through the midst of the merry-making
with the air of one who tolerates such things for
the sake of other people, but who has no personal
interest in them. This, at least, was his deport-
ment at home and with Sylvia. That he might
be different when out of her sight had not crossed
her mind. And if he was different, it was not
because he meant to deceive. Nobody was ever
less a conscious villain than Jocelin.

So he took the three women to the Atlanteans'
Ball, and handed them over to the reception
committee, and spent the rest of the evening
wandering over the opera house cursing his luck.
And the reception committee took Enid and
Sylvia and Jeanne, and put them down in the

seats just under the gallery, where all the other favored young women who were to dance with masquers were seated. The parquet, which had been boarded over for dancing, stretched out ahead to the curtain, and all around the pretty girls — such pretty ones, some of them! — were chattering and smiling, and pulling out their gauze sleeves, and nodding to acquaintances, and examining their programmes, and behaving just as pretty girls behave in their best gowns all the world over. Sometimes the words one caught were French, sometimes English.

"How nice it would be to be called Lu*lu*, with the accent on the last syllable!" said Enid, referring to an excited, black-haired little débutante who had been talking to Jeanne over the heads of three other people, gesticulating and laughing, and pretending to be in great distress of mind lest her masquer should forget that he had ever sent her an invitation.

Several "black coats," as they were called, to distinguish them from the Atlanteans, had already come up and put their names down on the lower half of Jeanne's programme. She was to dance all of the masquers' dances, and her less fortunate friends were congratulating her.

The band played at intervals; Sylvia began to look a little tired; the electric lights around the queen's box shot into being once or twice to make sure of themselves; and at last the queen and her maids appeared, and after a short delay the curtain rose on the first tableau.

"And there are millions and millions of girls who never experience this sort of thing, and never will," thought Enid.

Until this winter, she had never had the simple joyousness of a society girl's life so clearly put before her. She had begrudged wealth, books, comforts, for her poor people; she had wanted to give them music and art, but she had never before desired for them mere well-bred, civilized, butterfly enjoyment. She thought of her young garment-workers, — years older than these girls in experience, but no older as far as birthdays go, — and she wanted to turn all these pretty creatures out of the opera house, and let their serious, tired sisters in. The girls Enid knew were the respectable, hard - working poor ones, who liked better things, and could not afford to take cheap amusements, even innocently, because of their own reputations. Enid wanted to give them gay dancing and tableaux for once. She had never known herself so light-minded, so non-educative, before.

The pageant on the stage changed mistily, trap-doors came up; drop-curtains came down, and the happy, light-hearted crowd around said "Oh!" and "Ah!"

And then the masquers began to stream down from their various posts on the stage, and to

march two and two around the floor, while the
king and queen sat on their thrones at the back
of the stage in all the glory of electric lights
and tinsel. In another minute the front of the
parquet floor was filled with a crowd of quaint,
capering figures, Jeanne was disappearing from
view on the arm of a great ice-ghost, one of the
floor committee was taking Sylvia up to a respect-
ful sea-dragon, while a lively nymph with a tri-
dent was executing a Highland fling on a line
with Enid's vision, and pointing at her and
saying: —

"Yes, you! — you! Come on!"

And presently she and the sea-nymph were
dancing the Lancers in the same set with Jeanne
and Sylvia and Roma. In the middle of the
visiting figure the sea-nymph said, "Oh, I forgot!" and proceeded to pin a gold souvenir
brooch on her shoulder, thereby throwing that
figure of the Lancers into confusion for eight
people, who apparently thought it the greatest
joke in the world. When he took her back to
her seat, the sea-nymph gave her a lock of his
hair, as he expressed it, in the form of a long
strand of imitation seaweed twined with pearls.

Later in the evening, when she and Sylvia
were upstairs in a box resting, watching the
dancers, and drinking the lemonade which Jocelin procured, Jacques appeared, grinned in at
them, and mopped his face, saying: —

"Was n't I clever to get here so early? I almost lost my train, and I ran most of the way here from the house."

Indeed, he looked as if he had, for his face was scarlet and his hair was wet. Later he said:—

"That little sister of mine has had a fine time; she has n't been back to her chair once since the masquers came on the floor."

Enid wanted to ask him how he knew this, if he had only just come in, but she thought it was not quite fair to tease him.

Jocelin took Sylvia home early, and Jacques and Enid danced, and waited around till Jeanne was ready to go. Once, in their peregrinations over the opera house, they came upon Baird and Miss Campion comfortably ensconced in a *baignoire* in the "seconde."

"We're consulting about that dinner," said Baird, with a good-natured smile of dismissal.

"Yes, so I thought," said Jacques, and he added to Enid as she drew him away:—

"They've begun their housekeeping a little ahead of time. I wonder if she knows why he's giving that dinner?"

"I have n't told her," said Enid.

"I would n't give two bits for his chances with her if she does," Jacques remarked decisively. And then they went downstairs again to the floor.

Mardi Gras, when it came, was a fragrant,

breezy day, and, although Roma Campion sent
her carriage early for Enid and Sylvia, the two
women found the streets through which they
drove already alive with masquers. There were
children in parti-colored garments, darkies in
ticking coats and stove-pipe hats, wagon-loads of
men and women with banjos, guitars, concertinas,
and Jew's-harps. A wild horde of ragamuffins,
bold in their bravery of turkey feathers and red
paint, kept the carriage waiting five minutes
while they performed a war-dance in the middle
of the road. Nobody made any objections, or
told them to move on. Miss Campion's impressive colored coachman sat upon his box with im-
perturbable amiableness until the young rascals
got ready to clear the way.

It is not the élite of the city who dress up in
masques and run about the streets; it is the children and the "people," — close kinsmen these.
The fancy costumes are not always elegant, the
jokes are not always refined, but the gentleness
of sweet charity is abroad, and everybody laughs
and loves his neighbor. The very policemen on
the street corners "smile peace."

Enid and Sylvia spent a quiet morning in Miss
Campion's garden. Curtis Baird was there part
of the time, Jacques dropped in for half an hour,
other people came and went sociably. Several
old ladies, friends of Miss Campion's grandmamma, sat on the pillared gallery in a row,

waiting for the procession. When it came, everybody took a chair and ran down across the lawn to the tall iron fence, and everybody, old and young, mounted a chair and hung over the fence, and nodded and waved flirtatiously to the masquers on the floats, and dodged to escape the showers of hard candy.

After the procession had passed and the lap-luncheon had been served, Enid and Sylvia were taken home through the surging, good-natured crowds to rest before the dinner.

CHAPTER IV

CURTIS BAIRD GIVES A DINNER

THE dinner had to be an early one on account of the evening festivities; so, promptly at six o'clock, Jacques marshaled his party into Moreau's. Not downstairs, where the floor is neatly sanded and the tables are small and white, but above in a private room, where there were enough gas-jets blazing to have illuminated three rooms instead of one, and where there was a table laid for ten, a tablecloth and napkins crimped and crinkled marvelously, and an armchair at every place, because that is the fashion at Moreau's.

Curtis Baird asked Madame Dumarais to honor him by taking the end of the table, and every one sat down with a rustle and a buzz, — madame, with monsieur on one side and Jacques on the other; Curtis Baird opposite her with Roma and Jeanne; Enid next to Jacques, Jocelin next to her, then Roma; Sylvia next to monsieur; and between her and Jeanne a youth of the beard-less, susceptible kind, invited to balance the table, — a fact which he was fortunately incapable of grasping.

Everybody talked at once. And there were
raw oysters, and *gumbo filé* that hung all gluey
and thick from the spoon, and was full of oysters
and crabs and shrimp, and had to be eaten with
rice, of course. And there was *court-bouillon* of
red snapper with any amount of spices in the
tomato - sauce. And there was terrapin stew.
And there was *jambalaya*, that was rice and
beans and chopped ham and several other things
and pepper, especially pepper, all in one delicious hodge-podge. And there was woodcock
with salad, — and everybody knew the salad-dish
had been rubbed just once with a piece of garlic,
but it was excellent salad notwithstanding. And
there was white wine and red, and champagne.
And there was biscuit glacé in blocks, with exactly the same amount of strawberry ice at one
end of every block. And finally there was the
brûlot, which came in a bowl on a platter, and
was made of herbs and spices and something al-
coholic, and was ladled out into cups. But that
was afterwards, and that was the smallest part
of the pleasure of it, for first Curtis Baird stood
up and said : —

"Friends, — I have dwelt among you — a little
space, — and you have called me brother. I have
eaten of your *jambalaya*, and found it good. I
have drunk of your filtered rain-water" (there
was a shout of derisive laughter from the company), "and that, too, — was good. I have" —

He glanced sidewise down at Roma, lazy mischief lurking in the corner of his eye. She smiled, and her lips said voicelessly : —

"If you like."

Poor Roma! if she had but known what was to come after!

"I have — made love to — your women, — and they have found — me not altogether — unpleasing. I — I speak for one of them." (Great applause.) "Friends, — I have come to stay. The firm name is ' Baird & Dumarais.' Here's to Jacques; may he never desire a better partner — than myself, — ladies always excepted."

Enid and Monsieur Dumarais had known what was coming, but the rest of the company had expected simply the announcement of the engagement, and there was a gasp, and then a clapping and shouting and clinking of glasses. Everybody at one end of the table shook hands with Jacques, and everybody at the other end shook hands with Curtis Baird. Miss Campion's hand was unpleasantly cold, but a rigid society training is worth a good deal in an emergency of this kind.

After Miss Campion had been toasted, and Mr. Baird, the head waiter came forward, turned down the gas, and applied a lighted match to the *brûlot*, and all the bowl and the platter were set on fire, and there was a many-colored flame playing over the surface of the liquid. Everybody said "Ah!" and watched it in silence a moment, till Baird cried: —

"A song, — a song! Miss Castaigne! Mr. Jocelin!"

And back and forth across the table Jeanne and Jocelin sang one of the old creole folk-songs, verse and refrain, verse and refrain, sometimes one voice, sometimes the other, sometimes both together, — a queer, crooning, monotonous melody. And the flame in and around the bowl leaped higher and higher. First Jacques fell in with the refrain and the chant, then Roma Campion took it up, then Monsieur Dumarais, — backwards and forwards, up and down, crooning, chanting, swaying, till they all stopped, laughing and breathless, and the flame was at its height, leaping and curling madly.

Then Baird said: —

"Come, Jocelin, give us your best!"

Jocelin sat to the left of the blazing bowl, Sylvia diagonally opposite to the right of it, and Jocelin tossed his head back and laughed. Monsieur Dumarais bent his brows in an involuntary frown, and madame began to crumble a macaroon. Jacques, apparently unconcerned and at ease, nevertheless contrived, without attracting the attention of the company, to make an imperative sign to the waiter behind Jocelin's back.

It was not loud, that laugh of Jocelin's; it was only three low ripples, rich and thick in his throat, the kind of sound that flows across a listener's conscience and wipes off the value of the moral law.

It seemed to Sylvia that her heart turned over in her breast.

Jocelin's face was a devil's face on the other side of the weird flames, — a lean, brown, long-nosed devil, with all the blood of him in that red flower of a mouth beneath the faint black moustache, and all the fire of him in his eyes. How they blazed and beckoned, and said, "I am Sin," those eyes! And all the mad lost soul of him was in the sweet, seductive voice.

He lay back in his chair for a moment, thinking and humming softly. Sylvia watched the smile on his lips, and Sylvia's soul stirred through her body and felt the flesh of her, and rejoiced, and leaned out of her eyes.

"Oh, my God! It is not pity, — and I am glad! Jocelin, I am glad!"

On her own lips a smile trembled to dawn, but she did not know that she smiled, and her eyes had forgotten to look away from Jocelin's face.

This was how it was when Enid glanced across the table and saw her. The doctor's words came back to Enid. "Get her interested in something outside herself. Make her forget to think that she is thinking."

Well, the thing was done.

"I cannot bear it!" wailed Enid in her heart.

"Was there no other way than this? It is not true!"

"Ah! I have it!" said Jocelin. "Madrigal Triste."

He held his wine-glass aloft, and his hand was unnaturally steady. There was only a little wine in the glass, but the waiter appeared to be oblivious of the fact. Jocelin's eyes were wells of light, and his singing voice laughed, while beneath the gay song, hardly heard, were tears, the devil's tears.

"Que m'importe que tu sois sage ?"

he sang. The far-away look of thought went out of his eyes, and he turned to Roma, sitting beside him, and laughed into her face.

"Damn the fellow!" muttered Curtis Baird.

But Miss Campion did not notice. She had seen young men in the initial stages of exhilaration before. She was thinking of something even more disagreeable.

"Que m'importe que tu sois sage ?
Sois belle! et sois triste! Les pleurs
Ajoutent un charme au visage,
Comme le fleuve au paysage ;
L'orage rajeunit les fleurs."

He sang it to a mocking little melody which Jeanne had composed for some other song.

"Je sais que ton cœur, qui regorge
De vieux amours déracinés,
Flamboie encor comme une forge,
Et que tu couves sous ta gorge
Un peu de l'orgueil des damnés."

After this his voice seemed to leap forward, with no pause between the stanzas, and his eyes turned dreamily — was it by accident? — to Sylvia.

> "Mais tant, ma chère, que tes rêves
> N'auront pas réflété l'Enfer,
> Et qu'en un cauchemar sans trêves,
> Songeant de poison et de glaives,
> Eprise de poudre et de fer,"

> "N'ouvrant à chacun qu'avec crainte,
> Déchiffrant le malheur partout,
> Te convulsant quand l'heure tinte,
> Tu n'auras pas senti l'étreinte
> De l'irrésistible Dégout,

> "Tu ne pourras, esclave reine
> Qui ne m'aimes qu'avec effroi,
> Dans l'horreur de la nuit malsaine
> Me dire, l'ame de cris pleine.
> 'Je suis ton égale, O mon Roi!'"

He smiled exultantly and looked around on the company.

"I think that will do!" said Monsieur Dumarais. Baudelaire was not one of his favorites.

"Yes, that is the last stanza," observed Jocelin airily; "I omitted some of them, perhaps you may have noticed."

"And now, Miss Jeanne," interrupted Baird, fearing lest Jocelin should offer to sing the stanzas which he had omitted, which were, after all, the least objectionable, — "now, Miss Jeanne, where is that new song I heard you practicing not long ago?"

"Yes, Jeanne," said Jacques from the other end of the table, "sing the new one; sing Miss Sylvia's song."

Sylvia blushed, and everybody clapped, and Jocelin smiled across at her, a tender, protecting smile, an entirely unnecessary smile.

"I can sing it better standing," said Jeanne, and she arose.

The flames were beginning to die down a little, but they caught the yellow of her hair and burnished it, and sank into her innocent great eyes, and the shadows played about her white young throat. Once again in Jeanne's life her friends were to see her face looking out from flame; once again, at the end of her winter, the very end, — dear Jeanne!

"Turn up the gas," said Jacques abruptly; "this song needs light."

So the *brûlot* and the gas burned together, and Jeanne's rosy color came back to her cheeks in the brightness. She began with a joyous lilt : —

> "The young Spring came to the world
>   And found me!
>   And put her arm around me.
> And close — close — close — like rose-petals curled
> Up under a sheath — a sheath still furled,
> My heart at the heart of the young Spring's heart —
>   My heart — my heart —
> My heart at the heart of the young Spring's heart
>   Beat its music out, —
>   Beat its music out —

And the world —
Crowned me ! — crowned me ! —
Crowned — me !
And the world, — and the world —
Crowned me ! ' "

Dear little Jeanne, whom nobody ever crowned, — alas, nobody, nobody!

Her voice rang out in a perfect pæan of joyousness at the last. And oh, such applause as was heard in that private room at Moreau's!

Sylvia's health was drunk, and Jeanne's health was drunk, and in the confusion Jeanne found a moment to lean over to Sylvia penitently and whisper: —

"I am sorry we have not had time to write the music yet, Jocelin and I. You do not mind?"

In the end, at Jacques' suggestion, the gas was turned down again, and in the dim light of the rose and green and golden flames they all stood up, joined hands in a ring around the table, and sang "La Marseillaise" at the very top of their voices. The waiter came in in the midst of it and cried: —

"Messieurs, — mesdames, — the procession!"

When they heard him, they picked up anybody's wraps and rushed out of the windows upon the gallery. Enid wanted to get to Sylvia, but Jacques prevented her by almost garroting her with a fascinator and calling in her ear: —

"Come on! Come on! Don't you hear the music?"

Jocelin came to Sylvia's side of the table and put a shawl around her gently, and dropped a silk handkerchief over her head.

"Wait!" he said at the window, and pushed her lightly back with one hand, while with the other he lifted the window-sash higher. She stood almost within his arms for the moment, and she wondered if he felt her heart beat when he touched her.

"He can never know!" she said to herself, and she cried out against herself to tell him.

"Ah, bah!" said Jacques, leaning over the gallery; "it is a block off, and it has stopped. We might have finished that last song easily. Where is my father?"

He dived back into the darkened room.

"Come out, mon père, come out and stand by me while I tell you about them!"

Monsieur smiled with love and pride.

"No, my son. I have seen others; I know how they look. Go and enjoy yourself." And then, staying him: —

"Jacques, have you ever spoken to Mademoiselle Enid of Jocelin? Of what he — of how untrustworthy he is?"

"No!" said Jacques sharply, very sharply; "I do not see the necessity for warning Miss Enid against Jocelin."

Jacques could not see the gleam of amusement that flashed over his father's face, followed swiftly by a fixed seriousness.

"Set your mind at rest, my son," he said; "I did not mean that. It is her friend. I cannot see, but many voices speak to me. I sat next to Mademoiselle Sylvia at table just now. She is thrown much with Jocelin, as it happens, and Jocelin is very lovable. I think Mademoiselle Enid should know something of the life of the boy. She will see best how to employ that knowledge. It is not for us to warn her friend."

"Jacques! Jacques!" called Curtis Baird. "They are beginning to move again."

"I will tell her, my father," said Jacques, and went out through the window again to Enid's side. He still felt as if some one had said "Boo!" to him suddenly and made him jump.

CHAPTER V

BETWEEN FRIENDS

CANAL STREET was blazing with illuminations
of all colors, the banquettes were massed with
people, and the neutral ground in the centre between the two avenues was crowded with lines of
mule-cars. Down the street the brilliant pageant
moved with majestic slowness, in a cloud of
light. The floats swayed slightly, the figures
moved gracefully back and forth. The car with
Comus upon it passed the restaurant, and Comus
bowed and waved. Other cars followed. Dra-
gons, giants, Eastern temples, magic gardens,
demons, angels, dwarfs, fairies, drifted past. A
number of the men on the different floats knew
Jacques and spoke to him, and waved to Jeanne.
One called out: —

"The third dance is mine, you know!" and
threw her a heavy brass armlet hung with jin-
gling bangles.

Another shook his mace at Jacques and
said: —

"Nice floor committee you are! Why are n't
you down at the opera house?"

When the last float had passed, there was a rush and a scramble for one's own wraps, and a clattering down the stairs at Moreau's.

Sylvia was going home with monsieur and madame.

"Here! we'll put them in the carriage and then run for it; that's the simplest way," said Jacques.

Jocelin bowed at the carriage door and went off up Canal Street. He was evidently not going to the ball.

Miss Campion's grandmamma, who, with her glistening white hair and high-bred, clear-cut features, was handsomer than many a younger woman, was to meet the others at the ball and chaperon them. So they started two and two across the crowded street, — Baird and Roma, Jacques and Enid, Jeanne and the beardless youth.

Jacques was a master-hand at getting through a crowd; he had a way of saying "Look out!" in a blood-curdling, fire-engine sort of voice, when he approached a specially dense mass, and, after the scattering to right and left which invariably ensued, he and his companions fled rapidly down the alley thus obligingly opened for them.

Enid had one masquer's dance, but after that she was free, and she found Jacques waiting for her by the door of the parquet.

"You are tired," he said quietly; "I will call Jeanne."

"No, don't do that!" she begged. "Let the child enjoy her evening. Her dances are all engaged, and Lent begins to-morrow. She will not have another chance for some time."

So Jacques took her up to the proscenium box in the "seconde," on the opposite side from the Royal Box and above it.

"Now go away and dance your own dances; I will stay here quietly till Jeanne is ready."

"I have no dances engaged," he answered; "I am getting to be an old fellow, you know. I 've done this thing so often, the novelty has rather worn off. If you will allow me, I will sit here, too. Don't try to talk!"

They looked at the gay house and down upon the heads of the swaying dancers. Jeanne's head gleamed there, and once she turned her face straight up at them and smiled.

"It seems a little strange to me, Mr. Dumarais," said Enid, "that you, with your fondness for music and your fondness for Jeanne, should never have insisted upon her turning her musical gift to some account. It might be useful to her some day. One can never tell what straits one may be reduced to; and if she ever needed it, though I trust she never will, this power of making songs might help her to turn quite a pretty penny, even though her talent should prove too slight a thing to bring her what we call fame. Her voice, too, is lovely, and — and — forgive me if I seem to meddle, but I am fond of her, and we Boston women, who haven't as many men to depend upon as the girls have down here, learn early the need of being able to take care of ourselves. Jeanne, of course, has you now, but if anything were to happen to you? It seems cruel to leave such a pretty child unprovided for. And if you were to marry? She might find it irksome to be dependent, — she isn't your own sister, after all, and even own sisters object to being a burden upon their brothers."

"I thank you," said Jacques.

Perhaps, if he had analyzed his sensations, he would have discovered that he was chiefly grateful for the fact that she had not taken it for granted that he must marry Jeanne.

"I thank you. I believe it is quite true that we Southern men, with all our surface chivalry, do not always give our women a fair chance. But," he added, smiling down on the yellow head, "it's the very mischief and Tom Walker to make that butterfly of a creature study. She doesn't like it, you know, — never did. Jocelin worked at his voice, and she has constancy in her, too, bless her heart! but it all comes out in loving other people. I don't believe any other brother ever had a more faithful little sister than I have."

"Oh, you poor, blind, stupid man!" reflected Enid.

"She and Jocelin are like the two sides of a coin," Jacques continued. "There are the same characteristics in the metal, only they appear differently under the die. And she is the best side. You evidently take it for granted that Jocelin could not step into the breach, if I were put out of the way?"

Poor Enid was in no mood to say polite and pleasant nothings about Jocelin, but she controlled her bitterness and merely replied: —

"He seems to me too delicate in health to be relied upon as a prop in an emergency."

"A good deal of it is his own fault," said Jacques, "and yet, in a way, I suppose he could not help it. He is maman's favorite, and she did not know how to manage a boy. He was too near my own age for me to be able to interfere. I took him out into the courtyard and pummeled him well on one occasion, when we were boys, and he had been rude to my father, but that was the best I could do. And then there was the scandal about the opera singer. He has no pride. Perhaps you have heard that story mentioned?"

"He confessed it very sweetly to Sylvia, I believe."

It hurt her to say those words.

"Humph!" said Jacques, "I 'll bet he did. He was ashamed to come home for a while, and he got on pretty well till he got homesick and said he must come home. I wrote him he couldn't come, but he drew on me in New York and — he came home anyway. At least, that was the way I explained it to maman. I received a letter from a New York man with whom our firm has dealings, and he said, 'According to your instructions I have cashed the draft for your brother.' I was thunderstruck! And that day Jocelin arrived in New Orleans. I forced him to tell me. They were not my instructions, but he had signed my name to them. And, under the circumstances, what could I do? Of course I honored the draft for maman's sake. He said he could not remain there; he was dying of home-sickness. He has no stamina. The only grace he ever had was his voice, and he has wasted that. I have no sympathy with that sort of thing. But you might as well talk to a canary-bird as to Jocelin."

Jacques paused, looked down at the dancers, and then turned resolutely to Enid.

"Mademoiselle, it may be that I am going to displease you by what I say. Like you, I do not wish to meddle. I hope you will pardon me. Jocelin is very gentle, he is lovable, I believe, but he is not capable of making a woman happy."

Enid instinctively moved her chair so as to bring herself back out of sight of the opera house. She did not look at Jacques; she sat erect, and her nostrils quivered slightly.

Jacques felt alarmed, but he was not one to pause when he had convinced himself that a thing must be done.

"Your friend " —

Her face when he said these two words made him hold his breath for a second, such a flash shot from her eyes, such scorn and anger wreathed about her lips.

"Your friend," he faltered a second time, "thinks no evil. But she is sensitive. Jocelin is attractive to women. Of course you know her best. Pardon me! "

Her clear brown eyes seemed to cut straight through him. The majesty of the head upon the splendid throat made him ache. Her white breast rose and fell, but she kept her lips close shut for a long moment, and Jacques began to have a strained, buzzing sensation in his head.

"I thank you for your solicitude concerning my friend. You honor her by your inferences," she said at last, and the sound of her voice completed the sum of his wretchedness.

"You mistake me," he answered; "I meant no disrespect to Miss Sylvia."

"But you tell me your brother is weak, worthless, a scoundrel, and hint that my friend — my friend is attracted towards him."

"I said he was gentle and lovable."

"And that my friend is sensitive! You must be aware, Mr. Dumarais, that your brother's

faults are much more apparent, even to a dull
person, than his virtues are. What is it you
expect me to do? Do you think I will insult my
friend by telling her that I have no confidence in
her judgment and self-control? You should know
me better than to suppose that any one so dear
to me as Sylvia would be one to whom I could
say such things, to whom it would be necessary
to say such things. Yes, it is perfectly true that
I know her best. You should have saved your
warning, Mr. Dumarais, until you knew me better. I do not listen patiently to a disparagement
of my friend."

This constant repetition of "my friend" stung
Jacques' heart as the blows of a whip. Her
beauty, her championship of Sylvia, her ingrati-
tude towards him for his well-meant warning, all
maddened him.

"You shall not speak to me like this!" he
cried; "you know you are unjust. You know
I do not mean to insult you, — I, of all people
in the world. You turn my words against me.
I have made a mistake, but no mistake justifies
you in punishing me so cruelly. Am I to be the
only one who is to receive no consideration from
you? Is it all for her? — for her, whom not one
breath of mine has harmed? Your friend! your
friend! — but what of me? Have I not some
claim upon the rights of friendship, or do you
keep your pity and justice only for your women

friends? Do you think it has given me pleasure to hurt you? Would I not rather cut my tongue out than give you pain? And for a mere imaginary insult to a woman whom, of all women save you, I should least desire to injure, if only because — because you are so fond of her. For only a chimera, you grind me beneath your heel with such contempt! "

Poor Jacques! poor Jacques!

He was jealous. Enid, in the midst of her own heartache, recognized that and was sorry for him. The sense that he was not to blame smote her with remorse. She knew that she had turned her wrath upon him for the sake of shielding Sylvia, and that he did not deserve it. She knew that she had been perversely cruel, but she had not stopped to think how it might hurt him. And now she tried to make amends.

"I am sorry I have hurt you," she said gently. "But don't you understand? Don't you understand? It was not quite safe to tell me that the one who is dearest to me in all the world was in danger of giving her love to another, — and such a despicable other!"

"Do you mean it made you jealous?" said Jacques, quieting down, and speaking in a half-derisive tone, as if he felt his question too improbable to admit of being asked.

Enid flushed, but she felt that this was no time for half-truths.

"Yes, I mean just that," she said.

"But," he replied, looking rather amused, "it is n't the same thing at all. There would n't be any disloyalty in her doing it. Friendship is one thing, love is another. It is my experience that a love affair makes a woman rather more interesting to her women friends, — gives them something to talk about together. All women expect to marry."

"I do not expect to," said Enid. "My life has other work in it. And my friend is sufficient for me."

"You don't expect a man to believe that, do you?" said Jacques. He felt nettled.

"I expect you to believe it," she answered. "I want you to try to understand it, so you will be able to appreciate why I was so angry just now. If you loved a woman, you would not listen to such an insinuation any more than I do."

"Your loving a woman and my loving a woman are entirely different matters," said Jacques.

"You do not understand," she persisted.

"I understand enough!" he answered bitterly. "You have made part of your meaning very clear, — that I am not worth so much as your little finger to you, compared with your friend."

Enid meant to do the kindest thing, and his vehemence frightened her, so she said: —

"In one way that is quite true."

He sat still for a moment, and when he spoke his voice was not angry.

"It shall not be true," he said.

Just then some one pounded on the door, and Jeanne's voice cried: —

"Jacques! — let us in, Jacques! The door has caught on the inside."

And back upon his mind, like a blow, came the thought: —

"But, if I were in love with somebody else, would it be right to marry — which?"

Jeanne, Curtis Baird, Roma Campion, and the beardless youth trooped into the box.

"Awfully deaf, you two!" said Baird. "We knocked and knocked."

"We were discussing our friends," said Enid quietly. Her color was still bright. "That is always an absorbing occupation."

"Rex is coming, and we thought we could see better up here," Jeanne announced.

The three women crowded to the front of the box and looked down. They watched the Royal Party move slowly up to the back of the stage. They watched the stately courtesy of Comus and his queen towards the merry monarch who had condescended to grace their festivities with his presence. They watched the Royal Lancers dance with courtly precision and admirable management of mantles and trains. And who shall say how much they saw of it? Even Jeanne? This was the last ball of the season, and Jacques had not offered to dance with her.

"I shall go now," said Miss Campion; "I am tired," and in truth she looked rather white.

"We might as well all go," said Jeanne listlessly.

They went down together to the foyer and the vestibule, and when they were standing by Miss Campion's carriage, tucking in Miss Campion's grandmamma, upon whose physical strength the ball had apparently made no impression, Curtis Baird said: —

"Now we'll go home to repent us of our sins."

"Yes, to repent us of our sins," repeated Jacques dully. "Good-night."

Jacques always put out the lamp under the arch, so he kissed Jeanne and said: —

"You're dead tired, bébé; run to bed." And she went upstairs, but Enid lingered with him beneath the lamp and held out her hand.

"I am sorry we quarreled," she said, looking at him straight out of her sweet, wholesome eyes. "I was rude. I was unjust. I did not mean that our good comradeship had been nothing to me. It has been a great deal. It has been the happiest" — she paused and thought, "no, not the happiest, for Sylvia's new strength makes me happier, however it has come about;" so she corrected herself — "one of the happiest things the winter has brought me. I do not want to lose it."

This would have been an excellent opportunity

for Jacques to sulk, but Jacques was a gentleman.

"It was the thought of losing it which made me so miserable," he said, and he took her proffered hand. "When I am unhappy, I lose my temper. It is one of my failings."

"It is one of mine, too," Enid answered. "I thank you for being so generous."

"And you also."

Very late, Sylvia, lying awake, heard somebody coming along the gallery. He came slowly, and once he stumbled. He passed her door, and after he had passed she went over and leaned against it and listened. She heard madame's door open softly just a little way, and she knew that madame was standing watching him, but he did not turn nor stop; he went on along the gallery, and up three steps at the end, and again he stumbled, and turned off to his own room.

Sylvia lifted her arms above her head, laid them against the door, and pressed her cheek against the smooth panel.

"How I should loathe myself, if I were his wife!" she said.

CHAPTER VI

ASH WEDNESDAY was a warm, pale day; there
was no breeze to sway the branches of the big
magnolia-tree. The sunlight lay in the courtyard with melancholy quiet. And Jacques, on
a bench in a corner, was the stillest thing of all.
He sat with his elbows on his knees and his chin
in his hands. Enid looked down through the
gallery shutters and saw him there, and a quarter
of an hour later, when by chance she looked
again, he had not moved. She went into her
own room and closed the door softly.

Still Jacques sat in the courtyard, staring at the
sunshine on the bricks, — repenting of his sins,
perhaps; and if he heard Jeanne come down the
passage and stand beneath the arch, at least he
did not seem to hear her.

Jeanne said "O!" — a happy little round O, —
and Jacques lifted his head and smiled. But the
sunshine was just as sad as it had been before,
and the great white buds on the magnolia-tree
did not stir.

"Thou art not ill?" said Jeanne. She came

over to the bench and stood beside him, as a child stands, quite close.

"No, but there was nothing doing, so I came home."

He answered her in English. He had fallen into the way of speaking English to her since Enid and Sylvia had lived with them. There seemed to be less intimacy about it. Not that Jacques intended to be less intimate.

She was taking off her gloves slowly and looking down at him.

"And was last night's ball the best of all?" he asked presently, with something of an effort.

She sat down, began to pull out the fingers of her gloves, shook her head like a disappointed child, slowly, wistfully, and said : —

"N-n-o ! "

But he paid no attention to the hesitating monosyllable.

"Do you know, Jacques," she continued, "it was the very last of all the balls, that one, and you never danced with me a single time ?"

"Ah ! " said he, smiling, and pretending to be contrite. "Did I not ? That was a great oversight. Never mind. I will dance two dances with you next year to make up for it. But perhaps by that time there will be some other fellow, and your poor old brother will be left out in the cold. You may not care to dance with him."

"No ! " she cried impulsively, and the tears

came into her eyes as she tried to smile. "You tease, Jacques! Those balls have made me so tired! I don't like to be teased to-day."

"Eh, bien, non!" he said, and put his arm around her shoulders.

The knowledge that she was as yet unconscious of the meaning of her own feelings, and that any careless word of his might enlighten her, made him uneasy, frightened, — for her sake more than for his own, be it said, for she was dear to him.

She settled herself against his arm and laid aside her hat, saying contentedly : —

"I have not talked with you tout seul for such a long time! There are so many dinners, and parties, and other people."

And again he made no comment. He was looking absently at the wall above the water-jar. He was thinking of Enid's face with the light of the lamp upon it. He had been thinking of her face all day, the strength of the mouth, the sweetness of the eyes.

"Jeanne," he began quite irrelevantly a moment later, "how should you like to learn how to put your songs on paper and see them printed? How should you like to study harmony and thorough-bass, — and be a musician?"

"Study!" said Jeanne. "Oh, Jacques, but didn't I finish studying? All the other girls have left school. No, I don't want to, — please, Jacques."

"It would not be quite the same," he explained;
"you should go to Europe"—

"And you?" she asked.

"I? Oh, I should stay at home and make the
money."

"But, Jacques, you said you could not afford
it."

"That was some time ago. It is different
now; do you not see? I shall be in business for
myself, and I have promise of a good business.
The money comes easier than it did. Think,
mignonne! Paris — Paris — and Berlin and Vienna. You shall go if you will."

"Why do you want me to go?" she asked.

Such an uncompromisingly plain question!
How are you going to answer it, Jacques? See
her eyes, how grave they are, and her mouth,
how listless! Why did you want her to go,
Jacques, after all?

"Do you not love your music, little one?" he
said. "Do you not want to learn to use it well?
I think I have been thoughtless. Here is a great
gift le bon Dieu has given you, and I have done
nothing to help you use it."

"You have been talking to Miss Enid," she
said suspiciously. "Those are the things she
says to me."

"Miss Enid is very wise," Jacques answered,
smoothing the fluffy hair.

She only looked troubled and shook her head.

"Listen, my little sister. It might be that some day you would need money."

"But you always give me money, Jacques; I do not even have to ask for it."

"I know, I know, but listen. If I were to — die" —

He was afraid to say "marry."

She gave a little cry, and flung her arms around his neck.

"Why do you say such things? When I am so tired after the carnival, and this weather is stifling, and — you make me cry. I do not want to go anywhere but here. I should be homesick in another place, — in Paris, in Berlin, in Vienna. I will not go, Jacques. Why do you talk about dying? Is it not enough that this is Ash Wednesday, and the tears are so close to my eyes?"

He dried her tears and kissed her, but could not leave the subject alone.

"It is not fair to you to let you see so little of the world."

"There are other girls who do not see as much!" she protested. "There is Thérèse Bonet, — she never goes away. And I have been three times to the Pass, and once to Mississippi City, besides that time to Brown's Wells when maman was ill."

"You will be falling in love with some good-for-nothing fellow here, and only because you have not seen enough of other men," he continued.

She laughed quite merrily at this.

"Oh, funny! Do I look like falling in love? No, I shall stay here with you. I do not wish to go away. I will learn how to write Miss Sylvia's song soon. But all that is so slow, Jacques, and I do not want to do it — all the time, — all the time, nothing else! You are not going to die, Jacques. You do not feel a bit like dying. You only say that to tease me."

He thought of David Copperfield and Dora, and felt sick: In one way he knew the parallel did not hold good, for he should have nothing to complain of as to dinners and bills if he married this little creole girl. She was frugal by instinct and education; she had the true French talent for careful shopping. But was this all that he had a right to expect from marriage? — a good dinner, and after dinner a little wife upon his knee, to be petted, — eternally petted? Only this, when there were other women in the world who were made to walk with a man shoulder to shoulder? He thought he was tired of deciding all his affairs without help from others. Enid's word "comradeship" rang in his ears. He no longer said, "If I were in love with somebody else." No, he only said, "Which?"

"Then you will not go?" he asked slowly, as if he were thinking of something else.

"No, no!" she pouted. And then, with a sudden access of repentance, "If you wish it,

Jacques, I will go. I will study very hard. I
will if you wish it, Jacques,—Jacques!"

The tears were coming again. He could not
bid her go after that.

He sent her to her room comforted, and he
sat in the courtyard till the sunlight was all drawn
up over the walls, and the bricks were growing
damp, and the magnolia-tree had rustled once or
twice. Then he got up and went into the house.

Were you trying to buy her off, Jacques? Did
you think that that was one way out of it? Did
you really think so?

CHAPTER VII

THE COMING OF SPRING

And then the end of Jeanne's winter came, and Jeanne died. There was no warning; it was one of those great crashes that shiver unexpectedly through the harmony of God and offend men's minds as a discord. Who would have thought that Jeanne could die? But she did die, suddenly, terribly, one night in April, on the shore of the lake where she had played in her childhood, where Jacques had called her "little wife," and carried her about in his arms.

It was Jacques who had planned that they should all go across the lake and camp out over Sunday in the old house on the beach, so that Enid and Sylvia might have a glimpse of Southern country before they went home.

Enid wanted to go home in March, immediately after the carnival, but Sylvia's father wrote that the weather in Boston was atrocious, and as long as Sylvia was really gaining, a fact about which he seemed skeptical, she might as well stay another month. So what could Enid do?

She tried to forget herself in her economy

books as much as possible, for the things that went on outside of her grew more and more difficult to endure. But she had to stay. She had to see the color come to Sylvia's face, and the light to Sylvia's eyes, and stand outside the reason why, — she, who had dreamed that it was given to her from God, by right of love, to bring soul's health to her friend; she, whose whole personal life was — Sylvia! And Sylvia said no word.

She had to watch the result of her own unwisdom, too, — her own stupidity, she called it; she had to see Jacques conscientiously, miserably, striving to sacrifice himself for Jeanne's sake. She reviled herself for being heedless, and her heart ached for Jeanne, poor Jeanne! who was to be given the shell of the thing with only emptiness inside. Jacques' face was stern, and his chin was set hard. People thought he was intent upon his business affairs. Once Enid saw him turn away from the little sister with a weariness that had something of loathing in it. But he, too, said no word.

Finally, she had to witness the painful spectacle of a worldly woman coldly preparing to wreck her own life. As it happened, a wreck was averted, but that was not due to Roma Campion. She was ashamed to break her engagement, for she generously confessed to herself that this young man with the quizzical blue eyes had

not consciously deceived her. If he had shown
that he felt guilty, she could have freed herself
with a good conscience, but — she was ashamed
to be degraded in his eyes, and — she could not
make up her mind to let him go. Why? Was
it pride? Or was it something nobler of which
she was as yet unaware? Perhaps, for in the end
the wreck was averted, but there was one while
of storm. Enid saw the storm coming, but Roma
shut her eyes, bought her gowns, and was cold
and brilliant. Sometimes she would put hypo-
thetical cases to Enid, as: —

"If a man were to ask you to marry him, and
you didn't love him," etc.

But otherwise she, too, kept her own counsel.

And nobody was looking for such a thing as
death. Life seemed inevitable, painfully long,
wretched, and not to be escaped, to all of them
just then. To all except Jeanne. Jeanne had
so much joy in life!

The beach at that side of Lake Pontchartrain
is sandy and white, a good safe place for a bonfire if the wind is right. They couldn't wait for
a moon, because Enid and Sylvia were going
home in a few days; so they built a bonfire on
Sunday night and sat around it, talking of the
summer plans. Curtis Baird had a lodge in the
White Mountains, and they were all to "come
up" and be with him and "his wife" in August
or September.

They separated and wandered off in couples after a while, and madame went up to the house to prepare a late supper.

"I shall not be able to go," said Jocelin, with pathetic resignation.

"I think you ought to come back to New York and try to take up the work you left a year ago," said Sylvia.

Jocelin brightened. He wanted very much to be of that mountain party; it would be a pleasure to him, and Jocelin was fond of pleasure.

"I will consult with Jacques," he said more cheerfully.

There were several reasons why he would be obliged to consult with Jacques, — financial reasons. But Sylvia did not know; she only thought it very sweet of him to defer so entirely to his elder brother. She did not know how "little " the money was which, as he had told her, he earned by choir-singing.

They wandered along the beach slowly.

Jacques and Enid were sitting on the edge of the bath-house wharf, where it slopes up from the sand. Jeanne was putting brush on the fire. Roma and Curtis Baird had strolled down the wharf.

Jacques and Enid had their backs turned to Jeanne and the bonfire, and Jacques was saying: —

"I should like to ask you something. Do you

think Jeanne, — that is, you are a woman, perhaps you can tell me, — I should like to feel sure
before I — before I " —

He stopped a moment, and she felt sorry for
him, but she said nothing, so he began again : —

"She is such a child! You may have heard
people laugh about her preference for me, but
I am as a brother to her. I should not like to
startle her. She might think she must marry
me out of gratitude, and that would be such a
mistake! Do you think it wise for me to ask
her? "

He wished that Enid would show some distress,
some surprise, or confusion. If she had, there
would have been no more thought of Jeanne.
But Enid said: —

"I think she loves you with all her heart; you
only need to speak a word to her, and she will
understand herself. That will be the happiest
way for her to find out."

She had never before felt such full respect and
pity for this exemplary young man, who was trying so hard, so hard, to do his duty. And over
by the bonfire Jeanne began to sing, but Enid
and Jacques did not turn to look at her, nor did
they look at each other.

"Perhaps it will do no harm to wait a little
longer," he said.

"The young Spring came to the world,"

sang Jeanne.

Poor little deluded prophetess, whose spring never came!

> " The young Spring came to the world
>   And found me,
> And put her arm around me ;
> And close — close — close — like rose-petals curled
> Up under a sheath — a sheath still furled,
> My heart at the heart of the young Spring's heart,
> My heart, . . My hea — a — a — r-r "

Oh, the dreadful scream!

She had stood with her back to the fire, too close. And the flame swept up from her skirt to her head. She began to run. They always run. And she looked over her shoulder and saw Jacques running towards her, and the only thought that came to her clearly was: "It will burn Jacques!" So she ran faster, that he might not touch her, and she screamed: "No, no, Jacques! You will be burnt!"

It chanced that she ran away from the water along the edges of the gardens, and her dress caught on the fences as she passed and tore off in rags and burned there. She had a long start of Jacques, and the flames played about her feet like wings. She made no other sound after the horrible scream and the warning to Jacques, but he behind her was calling to her wildly to stop! to turn to the water! to wait!

"Jeanne! — Jeanne!"

He saw she did not understand him, did not hear him. She was past understanding anything

then. And as he ran, he knew that his running
only made her run faster, but he dared not stop.
He knew that, if he stopped, those terrible flames
could not be quenched. If he ran he was killing
her, and if he stopped he was killing her; and
the horror of it was beating up and down in his
brain and against the back of his eyes, so that
he could not see anything; he only ran on, debating the question as he ran, — stop? run? stop?
run? And that was not the worst of it, for back
of the knowledge that this was death came the
sense that there was nothing more loathsome in
life than to be able to have one's own way.
He hated all insistent, willful humanity, and
himself most of all. And he ran — stop? run?
stop?

Ten yards ahead of him, she fell down in a
gully, and went out like a torch. Then Curtis
Baird, who was a college man and an athlete,
ran past Jacques in the darkness, climbed down
the gully, and felt about in the water till he found
her.

Jacques lay face down on the sand, writhing,
not uttering a sound. And Baird, busy in the
ditch, found himself thinking : —

"It is the French excitable temperament. If
this thing had happened to Roma, I should have
felt as badly as he does, but I should have shown
it differently."

But Enid, standing stonily above the unmanned

creature on the sand, knew that this was remorse and loathing of himself, not love for Jeanne.

Jocelin sobbed like a child, and would not look at the little sister, would not touch her, crept shudderingly away when Curtis Baird lifted up the charred something that had been Jeanne, and carried it slowly up the beach and through the garden. For hours Jocelin wept; every fresh turn of thought brought the tears welling to his eyes. Later, when his childlike grief had quieted, the thought came to him that Jeanne could not be with them in the White Mountains the next summer, and then it occurred to him that perhaps, now she was dead, they would not go to the White Mountains. And he wept again.

Jeanne lived a few hours, if it could be called living, but they were all glad that she never knew anything more.

Madame, sitting by the table where they had laid the poor body, rocked herself to and fro, and cried, and stared about her helplessly. But the pity of it was that, when Roma Campion had come in ahead of the others to break the news, she had said: "There has been an accident" —

And madame had clung to her, white and flabby, and had gasped, "Not Jocelin?"

Poor little Jeanne! Poor little Jeanne!

Enid, stunned and weary, thought: "God is very good, for if, after she had become his wife, she had waked up to a knowledge of the emptiness of what he gave her, it would have broken her heart."

And Roma Campion drew a cloth over the face that had been so lovely, and said to herself: —

"I wish that I had died when I was nineteen, in the midst of the joy of it, even such a death as this. There are so many things that are worse!"

And she shuddered, but not for Jeanne.

Sylvia went away by herself to pray, and in the midst of her prayer the idea came to her that God might have done this thing for the salvation of Jocelin. If she could make Jocelin promise to write Jeanne's music and perpetuate Jeanne's name, for Jeanne's sake!

"He will do it for her. He is an idealist, and it will appeal to him and keep him steady, and give him a lofty purpose in life. And that will increase the power of his will. He will forget his own wretchedness."

A lofty purpose in life! This was Sylvia's idea of the need of Jocelin's temperament. She thanked God, and prayed for power to make Jocelin give his promise.

Oh, Jeanne, dear Jeanne! Was anybody sorry you died? Anybody?

Monsieur Dumarais groped his way into his son's room, where his son lay like a log on the bed.

"Do not grieve, Jacques. Do not reproach

yourself, my son. She never knew. She was happy always, and you gave her the happiness. She never guessed. And you would have married her. Do not reproach yourself!"

"The Almighty is terrible in his punishments!" said Jacques. "My God! If I had not rebelled against it, this would not be so horrible now, this being given my own way."

And monsieur was silent a moment before he said slowly: —

"Do you think you are going to have your own way?"

BOOK III

ON THE MOUNTAIN TOP

"Ici bas tous les hommes pleurent
 Leurs amitiés ou leurs amours;
 Je rêve aux couples qui demeurent
       Toujours."

                    SULLY PRUDHOMME.

CHAPTER I

CURTIS BAIRD'S HAPPY VALLEY

THERE is a little valley among the mountains of New Hampshire, — never mind where, never mind its name, — a little valley with a river winding through it, and great wooded hills bubbling up around, and in the blue beyond, peering up over the hills, two of the real mountains. The village in the valley by the river is one church-spire and a post-office, and the man who makes rubber stamps for post-offices cut the name of the village wrong on the stamp, but it was of no consequence, for they used the stamp just the same. And people who received letters from that village knew that one thing meant another, — or, if they didn't and were careless, they addressed their replies wrong and received them back from the Dead-Letter Office after several months. The real name of the village, not the name on the stamp, is the same as the name of the valley mentioned above, or was it mentioned? However, that also is of no consequence, you would not know it if you were told. Very few people know, and they only tell their intimate friends.

There is a long, white farmhouse under a hill on the opposite side of the river from the village, and the same summer boarders live in it every summer for generations. There is no bridge across the river nearer than the next town, so people have to ford the river, except when it is too high, and then they have to go seven miles around. When the summer boarders eat a great many blueberries with cream for tea, they dream that the villagers have built a bridge across the river. And that is a terrible nightmare.

Curtis Baird came down thirty miles through the wilderness from Canada one summer in his college days, and, standing in an open place on a ridge, he saw the valley far below, green and sheltered, with vase-like elms scattered over its meadows and the ribbon river looped about the hills. Curtis Baird had a nice taste for poetry in his college days, and always and forever he had a delicate appreciation of nature; but as he stood on the bare ledges at the top of the ridge, it took him some time to decide why this lovely intervale sank into his mind as the picture of a marriage festival, — why Spenser's marriage hymn seemed translated out of words by the river and the elms and the wind-ripples bending the long grass. The reason, or a part of it, came to him at last through the serene and swan-like curves of the trees, and he remembered how the swans came down the river in the poem. And, being a college man, he ruminated awhile upon the psychology of the impression and the queer tricks a man's mind will play him.

"Let us go down and take possession," he said to his chum.

But of course, when they got down they found that some one had been before them, for the long, white farmhouse was already there, under the hill, and so were the summer boarders, college professors, clever, mild-mannered men of culture, who glanced indifferently at Baird, and thought he would go away quickly to the other side of the mountains, where there were hotels and fashionable things. But they were mistaken. He stayed, and he came again year after year. He came in the winter, when the two tall, over-peering mountains, the guardians of the valley, were black against the sky and snow-streaked down the length of their ravines; when the forests on the lower hills were black, with sprinklings of snow along the tops of the pine trees, and the swift river flowed, invisible, beneath the white and sleeping meadows of the intervale.

He came in the spring, when the logs were tossing, tumbling, sliding, locking, down the swollen river, and the waterfalls were savage, and the bark on the young poplar-trees was green and alive with the new sap that rioted through it. He stayed late in the autumn, till the sunset lights

on the mountains were fierce copper and blood-
red, and the elms in the valley had yellowed and
dropped their leaves.

He built him a snug lodge in a high pasture,
with mountains stretching back behind him, and
the marriage festival of the intervale forever smiling below. And it was a favorite theory with
him, not mentioned to his chum, that when he
married he should bring his wife here and watch
her face to see if she, too, thought of the swans.
But she did n't think of them, because, you see,
he married Roma Campion, and she had never
read that particular poem of Spenser's.

Curtis Baird was married in June, but it
was not until after a honeymoon spent in the
Yosemite, and supplemented by a round of vis-
its among friends and relatives, that he at last
brought his wife up to the primitive lodge over-
looking the New Hampshire valley, and then it
was late August, quite time for the arrival of
Enid and Sylvia, and Jacques and Jocelin.

Baird had to wrestle with Jacques' Cotton
Exchange prejudices in order to make him come,
for Jacques said : —

"This is no way to build up a business, — to
have both partners gallivanting round the country at the same time."

"Hang the business ! " said Curtis Baird. "Do
it by telegraph. Work it through the New York
market. Can't you? That old duffer you 've

got at the desk looks steady enough to be trusted
with the secrets of a Turkish harem; and young
Brown, or Jones, or whatever his name is, had
practice on 'Change before you took him. He's
quite a lively hand at it. Thinks he is, any way.
He could n't wreck us in two weeks."

"That's all you know about it," said Jacques.

"You're too cautious," Baird persisted.
"Here you are working yourself to the bone, and
getting yellow and flabby, and all out of condition, and presently the heat'll knock you over
and you'll die. And here I'll be, with the business on my hands, and a fine mess; for what I'm
expected to do with it in such an emergency the
Lord only knows, — I don't."

"I'll take a run later, when you come back,"
said Jacques.

"And spoil all the fun," objected his friend.
"You're mopy, Jacques. It has been awfully
hard lines on you this spring, I know."

But he did not know in the least.

"Awfully hard lines, old fellow. I don't ask
you to come for the pleasure you'll get out of
the visit. But that mountain air will tone you
up, and make you feel like a different man.
We'll be all old friends together; you won't
have to bother about entertaining the girls, you
know. And my wife'll be disappointed if you
don't, Jacques. She's really awfully fond of
you. And she's quite set her heart on this little

reunion. You need n't be away more than two
weeks, all told, and we 'll get the telegraphic
market-reports every day, and the office can send
you a dispatch in cipher every night. Come on,
old man! don't be such a Miss Nancy. It 's all
nonsense to try to plan a leave when I get back.
How do I know when I 'll get back? May be
October, may be December. I can't pin myself
down to any set time, you know."

So Jacques promised to go, and forthwith set
about training young Brown, or Jones, or whatever his name was, luring him on with the hope
of a "rise" in October.

Jocelin's going required more tact and diplo-
macy. Jocelin had made up his mind that he
must go, that nothing was so necessary to his well-
being as this journey to the White Mountains.
He based the spiritual necessity upon the fact
that Sylvia had said to him when she went
away : —

"I am going to ask you to make me a promise,
when you come North in the summer, a promise
for Jeanne's sake and your own sake, — and
mine."

The memory of Sylvia's face, as she said these
words, remained long in Jocelin's æsthetic consciousness. He wanted to see her again, — just
for the pleasure of watching her beautiful eyes.
And stronger than this was the desire to be idle,
and enjoy Curtis Baird's good wine, and lie out

under the trees for a while with a beautiful world above and around, and no need to work and attend choir-practice, and make untuneful pupils sing the scales.

The sense of the nearness of a beautiful woman remained always a part of the picture in his mind, but never overshadowed it. Jocelin was a worshiper when in Sylvia's presence, but, like some other worshipers, he left his emotion at the door of the sanctuary. Sylvia absent was a pleasant memory, — something that he was as yet glad he had not lost the right to look upon again.

But Jocelin had no money. He was even feeling rather pinched for funds just now; he had not Enid's and Sylvia's board to fall back upon when he got himself into a tight place. And therefore it was that, in the latter part of June, he took to loitering in his mother's sewing-room, — such a sober, dreary place now that Jeanne's pretty finery no longer littered the chairs and the floor. Jocelin would lounge idly in one of the chairs, snipping up little pieces of black Henrietta cloth, or pushing the pins up to their heads along the ridges of his mother's symmetrical tomato - pincushion. Sometimes he would say moodily: —

"I can no longer endure this life. It is killing me, this living in the same house with Jacques and eating his bread. I will no longer suffer this degradation. I must go away."

Then the pulpy organ which the doctors called madame's heart would so comport itself that, for the next fifteen minutes, madame would be all splotchy, and perhaps she would weep a few slow-squeezed tears and say tremulously: —

"Oh, my son, my Jocelin! It is not possible that thou wilt go away from me! Thou art not so cruel! And thy sister is dead! Thou wilt not leave me, too?"

And Jocelin would proceed to enlarge upon his family pride, his sense of unbearable degradation. He complained at these times of being tied to his mother's apron-strings; he dwelt in mournful retrospect upon the large sums paid by New York millionaires for parlor singers. He even hinted darkly at some tragic event which might transpire if he were forced to remain much longer beneath the same roof with his successful and domineering step-brother.

At other times Jocelin would sit for an hour or more in the sewing-room, absolutely silent, staring wistfully into space, sighing occasionally the softest, most pathetic sighs.

"Tu ne te portes pas très bien aujourd'hui, Jocelin?"

"Oui, Maman, assez bien, comme toujours."

Jocelin was no more conscious of deliberate scheming than a child is when it wheedles for a cooky. Jocelin wanted this pleasure very much indeed, and it was his nature to do all in his power to get what he wanted. It was Jacques' nature, too, for that matter; but Jacques did not want the same things, and went about getting them differently.

Madame endured this torture for a month. Jocelin did not know it was torture. Perhaps he would not have persisted in it, if he had known. Perhaps. And at last, in July, madame went to Jacques and laid the case before him, dwelling upon Jocelin's ill-health, immense pride, hatred of dependence, desire to redeem himself and prove himself more worthy of respect, — in fine, his wish to go to New York and try to win back the position he had been on the way to acquiring two years before.

Nobody could have put the case better than madame, for nobody ever had less logic than she to bring to bear upon her idolatry.

"Do you want him to go?" asked Jacques in his quick, decisive way.

Madame did not want him to go in the least, but he had set his heart upon going, and she was his mother. She pleaded babblingly for his desire.

He was making himself ill over his uselessness. He was brooding over it, and he was so sensitive, so high-strung! It might be — here madame fidgeted her scissors and avoided Jacques' eyes — it might be not so bad if — if — It was quite evident that Mlle. Sylvia was attracted by Jocelin; he was lovable. Had not madame understood that Mlle. Sylvia was rich? It might be more of a help to Jacques than an expense, in the end, this journey.

Jacques' first thought was a pleasant one: "If she married, my own desire might prosper." But he thrust it from him, and said sternly: —

"You have not mentioned this to Jocelin?"

No, madame had not mentioned it, — that is, she thought she had not.

"Then please do not do so," Jacques commanded.

And madame, suddenly recalling an occasion when she had hinted such a possibility to Jocelin, became clammy with cold perspiration, but did not correct her misstatement. Instead, she veered to another line of appeal.

Jacques had intended to take Jeanne North this summer; would he not, therefore, use this money for Jocelin? It would mean no more expense. Jeanne would have been the first to plead for her brother. No doubt she wept now in heaven at the sight of him so pale and discouraged. If Jacques would allow madame to do this thing as a memorial for Jeanne? Jocelin would die, assuredly, if something were not done. His father was that way, speechless and melancholy, the year before he died. For Jeanne's sake!

And so, in memory of Jeanne, Jocelin was sent to perdition at a slightly accelerated pace.

That mountain air, of which Monsieur Baird spoke favorably, would perhaps prepare Jocelin for his winter of work. And Jacques would keep Jocelin with him as much as he could in the North.

The tone in which she made that last petition betrayed madame's wretchedness.

Yes, Jacques would keep his eye on him as long as he could. But this must be understood, — there should be no coming home unless he paid his own way. Maman was not to get ill and fret.

All of which maman promised, and further obtained that the money should go to Jocelin from her, for Jocelin was so proud, so sensitive! If he were aware of this new indebtedness, he would assuredly refuse to go.

So Jacques and Jocelin went North together, preserving the same degree of *camaraderie* as might have been displayed by two unfriendly convicts chained to the same ball. They arrived at Baird's lodge about the middle of August.

Sylvia was already there, having come from her brother's house at Beverly Farms.

Sylvia's brother's wife was puzzled. She said to her husband : —

"I never did pretend to be able to understand Sylvia, but since she has gotten better, she is more inexplicable than ever. Do you suppose she is in love?"

And Sylvia's clever brother laughed, and said: —

"No fear of that. Too much Enid."

Sylvia greeted Jocelin with a remote gentleness that made him more worshipful than ever.

The next day Enid came from a small town in western Massachusetts, where she had been visiting her nearest surviving relative, a maiden aunt, who had sent her through college and regretted it ever since.

"Just a good number," said Curtis Baird. "Three and three. We can go up on the mountain top some night and camp. The lean-tos hold three and three comfortably."

And Enid thought of Jeanne; and that old-fashioned counting-rhyme children say when they want to find out who is "it" came whimsically to her mind: —

> "One, two, three, four, five, six, seven,
> All good children go to heaven."

Dear Jeanne, left out in heaven!

CHAPTER II

THERE was a total eclipse of the moon that summer in August, three days after the arrival of Curtis Baird's guests.

"We'll go up the mountain," he said, "and watch it. I've never seen a total eclipse. Have you, Jacques?"

Yes, Jacques had seen one once when he was a little boy; he remembered being routed out at midnight to look at it. Or, no! he believed that was a comet. Perhaps he had not seen an eclipse, after all. He did not seem to care whether he had seen one or not; he showed remarkably little interest in the phenomenon, that is, remarkably little for him. He was graver than he used to be, and there was the shadow of a permanent wrinkle between his brows.

Indeed, if Curtis Baird had not been very fond of these friends of his, he might have found them all rather dull company just now. He thought they mourned for Jeanne, and they did to a certain extent; but each one had his or her own private preoccupation, which went deeper than any feeling any one of them had for Jeanne.

"We'll take them up and give them a night out of doors," Curtis Baird said gently to his wife. "There's nothing like Nature for a comforter. A night under the stars sets me up better than any tonic."

"Does it?" said Roma, without looking at him.

"Dear, do you think it's good to let your mind dwell so much on that little dead girl?" he asked, and added wistfully, "I know you were awfully fond of her."

"Yes, I was quite fond of her," she answered coolly, "but my mind doesn't dwell upon her very much. The accident was dreadful, but it was all over in such a hurry, you know, and I was some distance away."

"Don't you like the idea of this camping out?" he asked after a moment.

And she answered absent-mindedly, "Oh, yes."

It was only a little mountain, a climb of an hour and a half, but it had an open top and a view, and was well worth doing. At least, so Curtis Baird said. He had to supply enthusiasm for the party, and the rôle of the enthusiast was a new one for him.

The air was still and sweet that August day. The small brook pattering across the mountain path was full of water. Jocelin pulled up a long green vine that ran upon the ground and twined it about Sylvia's white woolen cap.

"That 's the linnæa, or you may call it the twin-flower, if you like," said Baird.

They rested often for Sylvia's sake, and because Baird said all good mountaineers went slowly and stopped often. They stopped once in a beech-wood, full of rosy and amethyst lights, bewildering to the town-bred Southerners, and Curtis Baird made Jacques lie down flat and look up at the bright sky through the leafy tracery.

They stood a moment at the foot of the ledges, and, through an opening in the trees, they had their first sight of the great mountains beyond, twenty miles away, with the late afternoon haze upon them. Then they scrambled up the ledges, laughing over their scramble till they were all in a glow, and by the time they reached the little cairn of stones upon the summit their dullness was gone.

"That at the far end of the valley is Cherry Mountain," said Curtis Baird. "You can even see the slide down one side of it, — do you see? And there are the great ones."

They looked a long time at the great ones, four in all, one pointed and sharp on the sky-line, one gently pyramidal, one low and lightly curved, and one, the highest of all, a great billow swelling up to the sky.

Roma Campion had a conventional and comparatively intimate acquaintance with the Alps, but Jacques and Jocelin came from a flat country; mountains were new to them.

Jacques took off his cap, threw back his head, and when, after a moment, he turned his face to Enid for sympathy, he was smiling. There was more of the vivacity of the old Jacques about him than there had been for many a day.

Jocelin stood .on a rock and looked far, far away to those shining mountains, and sang the one hundred and twenty-first psalm. Sylvia had never heard him sing so well. Sweet and full and solemn rose the music, winging from his lips out to those listening hills that lifted up themselves all bloom-impurpled by the dying sun.

" I will lift up mine eyes unto the hills, from whence cometh my help.

" I will lift up mine eyes, I will lift up mine eyes, unto the hills, the hills, from whence cometh my help.

"My help cometh even from the Lord, from the Lord who hath made heaven, — heaven and earth." . . .

All these people knew Jocelin very well, and they were none of them devoid of a sense of humor, and yet it did not seem to impress them as humorous that Jocelin should stand on the top of a little mountain at sunset and sing the one hundred and twenty-first psalm, — sing it with the reverence and the sincerity of a seraph.

But there was a great deal of humor in the situation, notwithstanding.

Pink clouds drifted about in the sky, the sun

went down behind the hills, and the valley far below drowsed in the twilight.

"I am awfully hungry," said Jacques.

Curtis Baird made the coffee in a villanous black coffee-pot, Jocelin cut the bread, Roma made sandwiches, Sylvia laid the viands out on a flat rock and trimmed them with leaves. Jacques brought pine and hemlock and spruce to Enid, and watched her make spring-beds in the two open camps. Then they all sat around the flat rock and ate their supper, and watched the mountains and the valley sink away from them into darkness, leaving them shut out from the world, till the large round moon rose on the other side and lifted up the valley a little way out of the abyss and set it smiling silverly, and beckoned the mountains from the darkness, but only a little way, for they stopped and stood aloof mysteriously, great shadows.

Curtis Baird unrolled the shawls and camping-blankets, and made his wife put on her jacket.

"And you have spent nights all alone on the top of this thing?" said Jacques. "What a queer fellow you are!"

The small supper-fire had gone out, and Baird was piling up great birch logs and putting pine branches on top.

"Not going to have a fire?" said Jacques uneasily.

"Of course," returned Baird. "What did you

suppose? Always have a camp-fire. Takes the
chill off in the middle of the night."

Jacques squared his chin and thrust his hands
into his pockets, but said nothing.

It was a beautiful fire, just between the two
open camps, — the lean-tos made of stones with
boughs laid over for the roofs, — open to the fire,
the moon, the rain, too, if it chose to come down;
but the clouds were gone, and the moon was sail-
ing in a clear sky.

Three and three they gathered around the
crackling flames.

"We might tell ghost stories?" suggested
Baird.

Jacques gave a stifled exclamation; it sounded
like "My God!"

"Let's get away from this!" he said a moment
later in a gasping voice to Enid, who sat next to
him, and she arose at once.

"I — we — we'll go and look at the moon for
a while," said Jacques to Baird. "Fire's hot,
— get a little air." He was still gasping and
trying to control his voice as he turned his back
on the flames and followed Enid across the rocks.

"I wouldn't have believed I could be such a
fool!" said Curtis Baird slowly. "Poor old fellow! Roma, why didn't you give me a hint?
What an unlucky speech!"

CHAPTER III

JACQUES AND ENID

THE place where Jacques and Enid went was a broad, sloping ledge covered with a deep lichen, pale green and pale lavender that had turned silver under the moon. The smiling valley was no longer at their feet, for they were on the other side of the mountain. They had come upon the wilderness, and they looked down on thick tree-tops everywhere. Over the edge of the ledge a ravine sank away, black with mystery; and opposite, above them, the shoulder of a near mountain loomed huge and austere, the untrodden forests on its sides silent and absolutely still in a moon-begotten sleep. The place was all wildness and solitude. Far below, something crashed in the bushes, and the stillness came again.

Enid and Jacques sat down on the dry, crisp lichen and looked out over the wilderness.

"I can't be making a fool of myself like this," said Jacques; "it won't do. But it was the first out-of-doors fire I'd seen since — since — And it brought it all back to me."

Enid said nothing. She was glad to have him

talk of Jeanne; she felt safer when he talked of
Jeanne, but she was afraid of something else.

"I miss her," he continued. "I did not know
I should miss her so much, but it appears she
was everywhere in that old house, and now she
is nowhere! Her hair! was it not the brightest
hair? Once I saw the sunlight against the wall
in the courtyard, and for a second I forgot and
thought it was her hair. She always came to me
when I entered the house. She was my child
from the beginning. I miss her, because she
was always near, as a child is near."

"I am glad, — glad that you miss her," said
Enid.

They were speaking softly, because the hush of
the forests compelled them. Enid discovered
that, when Jacques spoke low, his voice was deep
and almost gentle.

"I miss you, too," he said.

His tone was dangerous, and she hastened to
reply with a polite and cheerful inflection.

"I am very glad of that, also."

"I felt at first, when she died, as if I were a
criminal," he resumed. "It was an entirely new
sensation. It was horrible! I believe I must
have behaved like a maniac that night. I do not
remember. I had been so unsettled, so disturbed,
so unhappy, for a long time before. You did
not know that?"

She did not answer. She thought perhaps he

would go on without waiting, but he repeated his question wistfully: —

"Did you know?"

"Yes, — I knew."

She was so sorry for him, and she was not used to dealing with men. She wished at once that she had said something else, had temporized, had asked him why he thought she ought to know. She was a New England woman and a woman's woman, and her habit of sympathy had betrayed her; for this was no perplexed and over-spent college friend, or working-girl, who needed to be comforted: this was a young man, apparently on the verge of saying intimate and solemn things to her, which she felt she ought not to allow him to say. But how to prevent it now?

Jacques himself had not planned this conversation. He only loved her, and it was in the course of nature that he should tell her so some day. He had not supposed it would be this day, but it apparently was, so he proceeded to fulfill his destiny.

He fulfilled it with dispatch; that was Jacques' way. He said tenderly: —

"I love you! I want you to be my wife."

"That is absurd!" said Enid.

She answered lightly, but she wanted to laugh and cry. She was twenty-nine years old, and this was the first time any man had ever told her he loved her, had ever asked her to be his wife.

This was the great feminine event of her life, and she was deeply moved and excited, but all the answer she had at her command was, "That is absurd!" delivered in a polite, afternoon-tea sort of tone. The hysterical tumult within her made her eyes fill with tears and her lips twitch smilingly, but she turned her face from Jacques.

His eyes flashed.

"I lost my temper once when you were unjust to me. I shall not now. Why is it absurd?"

"Because we live in different worlds."

"Do we?" He looked bewildered.

"Yes!" she said. "Yes!"

. "But I love you," said he.

He said it so sweetly! There was something so wholesome about him! She wanted to pat him affectionately, as she would have patted a girl. But the situation demanded another course of action.

"You would not love me very long," she replied.

"You do not know that."

"True! I do not know, but I think so."

"I know," he said, speaking slowly, "that you do not love me. But you like me very much. Is not that true?"

"Yes, very true."

"Then do not say No. Let me try to make you love me. I only liked you very much at first, but now I love you. Give me leave to try."

"It would not be of any use."

"You do not know that."

"Yes, that is one of the things I do know. Listen! and I will tell you something about my life. You think you understand the real me, but you don't. No, really! Do not be angry."

He smiled and leaned towards her, looking steadily at her with his determined gray eyes, and saying: —

"When you have finished, however, I shall continue to think just as I do now. I shall continue to love you."

She had a hopeless feeling that what he said would prove perfectly true, but she shook her head at him with equal determination, smiling in her turn.

They looked at each other so for a moment, he compelling, she resisting, and that bright smile in the eyes of both. Then Enid turned away with a sense of effort, and weariness of the struggle to come.

The great sweep and slope of the mountainside lying beyond the ravine in the moonlight rested her, freed her from the strain of Jacques' insistent human nearness, and she kept her eyes upon it as she talked. The moonlight glistened on her heavy coils of hair and outlined the statuesque pose of her head and the large, classic correctness of her profile. A glow crept into her face as she talked. She was a pure joy to look

upon; she would be a warm delight to touch.
She forgot to look at Jacques, and it was just as
well.

"I am going down to the city next week to
begin to live my life," she said. "I am going
down to a little court that opens into a narrow,
crooked street, that opens again into a sticky,
smelly, crowded thoroughfare. And I am going
to live there, or thereabout, all the rest of my
life."

Her voice was very quiet, but there was something more than moonlight shining to make her
face so radiant.

"The people on the floor above me are a widow
and her son and daughter; they have lodgers.
The people on the floor below are a carpenter
and his family. There is a garment-workers'
shop in the garret. An actor and his wife and
babies live in the cellar. I know the widow
and the actor's wife. It is a respectable house,
and Sylvia has obtained permission to spend
the winter there, so her father has seen to the
plumbing."

Jacques moved restlessly, but Enid kept on.

"I shall go from there to my teaching, and
lecture-classes. Sylvia, if she is well enough,
will write. Perhaps," — her mouth curved be-
witchingly, — "perhaps, after a while, if I live
long enough and fully enough, I shall write a
book of statistics and social theories. I think I

can earn something by social essays in the maga-
zines now and then. I wanted to do this last
winter, but Sylvia needed me first, and I went
with her. I wanted to do it this summer, but
my aunt, who brought me up, needed me for a
little while. Now I am free to live as I was
meant to live. I will not be withheld any longer.
I do not want to marry you."

"You could still do your charity work if you
married me," said Jacques. "The married women in New Orleans are always busy over that
sort of thing."

"Charity work!" smiled Enid. "I told you
we lived in different worlds. This is not charity
work that I expect to do; I have no scheme, no
plan of action. I shall get up in the morning
and go to my work, along with all those others
who are earning their living. I shall only live
there, that is all. Perhaps in summer I may
come sometimes up here to these unpeopled mountains. I should like to come, and sit here at
night with some one who has never known the
meaning of solitude. I should like to come.
Ah, is it not beautiful, that mountain wall with
its dreaming forests? I know you do not understand what I am trying to tell you; I know you
do not understand, because it is the thing that
goes deepest into my heart, and there are no
words as deep down as that. How can I make
you know the reality of it? The world has spat-

tered us all over with words, with cant phrases, with sarcasm, and with fulsome flattery. The world has been so officiously eager to explain for us the thing we mean and the worth of the thing that now, when we try to speak, our meaning is veiled, concealed, smothered, by the hideous volubility of facile expression. How can it have any reality for you when you hear only words about it? Listen! I could not live with you in peace and plenty when there were people who swarmed in cellars, and had not the price of a crust of bread among them. And that is a cant expression. Get at the life-meaning, the heart of it, if you can."

"You should have as much money as I could spare, to give away as you pleased," said Jacques. "You would have more to give away than you have now."

She smiled ironically.

"Money that you have made by gambling in cotton futures for other people? Money that you have made by ruining one man in order to surfeit another? Oh, no!"

"That is all nonsense!" said Jacques. "I buy and sell cotton for my clients at the best possible advantage for them, and at a fair rate of commission. That is business. The firm never speculates. A woman does not understand these things. Business cannot be conducted on sentimental principles."

"If I were a girl," said Enid, "and if I were in love with you, I suppose it would be easy for me to shift the responsibility of these questions upon you, and rely upon your judgment, and my own conviction that you are an honorable man, — for that is my conviction."

His eyes lighted tenderly, and again he leaned towards her, but she continued without looking at him: —

"But a girl's love is not a woman's love; above all, it is not a modern woman's love. I, at thirty, cannot accept your views, adopt your methods, and believe your heresies, as you might be able to teach me to do if I were eighteen, — and if I loved you. I have found out my own life-truths, and they do not accord with yours."

"A husband and a wife are comrades," murmured Jacques; "they modify each other. You should not find me adamant to your convictions if you married me, for I love you."

"But I don't love you."

"Not now! Not now! But it is not an impossibility that you should love me."

She shook her head.

"Can't you understand? I do not want to marry you. I shall never want to marry you."

"I want you," said Jacques; "I want you! You have spoiled all other women for me."

"We do not touch," she answered. "I do not see why you love me. A husband and a wife confide in each other, live at the heart of each other. But we do not. You, who tell me I may have money to spend in charity; you, who expect me to live with you and ignore your methods of supporting me, your methods of dealing with your fellow-men, — do you think you get near the heart of my life? Why! My life is just that; it is my fellow-men. And I, — see how ignorant, how unappreciative of you I am, for I do not even know what your central effort is, the thing you are striving for. What is the heart of your life?"

"It is you!" he said simply.

Her heart jumped, and she sat very still for a moment, then bowed her head upon her knees. When she lifted her face and looked out once again over the ravine, there were tears in her eyes, and they caught the moonlight.

"I could not make you happy," she began, but he interrupted her with: —

"Let me judge of that!"

"No, no! There is something else you cannot understand. I do not need you. It is true I have no man friend whom I enjoy as much as I do you, but I have a woman friend who is dearer to me."

"But I told you once before, that is different," insisted Jacques.

"Yes, I know you told me," she answered; "but I know my own heart. I share with her thoughts that I have no wish to share with you. I give to her a love surpassing any affection I could teach myself to have for you. She comes first. She is my friend as you can never be, and I could not marry you unless you were a nearer friend than she. You would have to come first. And you could not, for she is first."

"And this is all that separates us?" said Jacques, in a tone of entire amazement. "Only a woman?"

"The reason the woman separates us," said Enid, "is because the woman and I understand each other, sympathize with each other, are necessary to each other. And you and I are not. It is not simply her womanliness, it is her friendship. There might be a man who could give me the inspiration, the equalness of sympathy, I find in her, — there might be, — some women find such men. But there are not yet enough for all of us."

Jacques got up and paced the ledge.

"You — you are noble!" he said.

He came back presently and sat down beside her as before.

"She is very delicate," he began angrily. "Have you ever thought how alone you would be if she were to die?"

"She will not die!" whispered Enid. "Oh, she will not die! Not now. She is getting well."

He did not understand the anguish in her voice, the wretchedness in her eyes, but something made him lean forward and say : —

"If she were to marry?"

Enid's face grew gray like the rocks of the ledge. She did not turn her eyes away this time; she kept them fixed stonily on him.

"Well?" she said.

And he had no reply to make.

"I am going to live down among the people who have next to nothing," she resumed after a pause, speaking in a natural voice. "I cannot make you understand by words. Perhaps some time I may make you understand by life. And, for the other, my own private and personal happiness, or unhappiness, — that you cannot alter, you cannot influence. My sorrow is only symbolic of the great world-sorrow, after all. I trust I shall not overestimate any personal grief which may come to me. And I know that the best way to keep myself free from self-pity and morbidness is to live in the presence of a greater sorrow than my own. And then, when I behold the full cup of bitterness the world lifts daily to the lips of God, I trust I shall be ashamed to add the little drop of what, in weaker moments, I call my suffering, to such a dignity of overflowing pain. Come, let us walk a little."

"You know I do not give up now," Jacques

reiterated; "I shall come back after a while, after
you have lived as you say. I shall come back
to see if I understand, — or if I can make you
understand."

"Better not!" she answered.

CHAPTER IV

"So you and I are to change places, are we, Jocelin?" said Curtis Baird, as the four sat around the fire after the abrupt departure of Jacques and Enid. "You are to turn New Yorker, and I am to take root in Southern soil?"

"For pity's sake, don't talk about taking root!" exclaimed Roma; "it gives me cold shivers."

"Queer!" meditated Baird; "such a hot place, you know. What are the prospects for New York, Jocelin? Anything definite?"

"No," replied Jocelin, with graceful nonchalance; "I shall look around. I shall visit the choirs."

"Rather early in the season for soirées, receptions, that sort of thing, is n't it?"

"Yes," said Jocelin musingly, as if the question had no practical connection whatever with the fact of his coming North at this unseasonable moment. "Yes, I believe it is."

Sylvia had risen, and was looking off towards the valley.

"How lovely! I should like to go and look at it for a while."

"May I come, mademoiselle? I will bring shawls," said Jocelin.

"Take that brown blanket with the blue border, in the left-hand camp," said Baird, with some alacrity. "Better get Roma's steamer-rug, too. The flat ledge where we ate our supper gives the best valley view. That's right, — the gray rug. May want a cushion. Good-by. Half past nine now. Eclipse not till eleven. Look out for Miss Sylvia going down to the ledge, — pretty slippery."

These remarks were addressed snatchily to their retreating figures. When the two were fairly out of sight he said: "Bless you, my children!" with a devoutly gratified expression of countenance, and proceeded to throw birch logs on the fire and make it crackle with pine branches. Then he came and sat down beside his wife, — quite close beside her.

"Jolly, isn't it?" he said.

She did not answer.

"Don't you like it here, Roma?"

"Yes," she replied gloomily.

The fire blazed merrily, lighting up the gay blankets that hung within the two camps.

"When do we go South?" asked Roma.

"Why, my dear, I don't know exactly. I'm afraid we ought not to put it off too long. That energetic Jacques is getting restive. Says he'll

throw up the whole thing if I don't give it some
personal attention. Says he can't run it alone;
needs somebody in the office, you know. When
I try to convince him that I am about as useful in
the office as a pug dog, he gets huffy. Says he's
not an object for public charity, and he won't
use my money unless I know how it's being used.
Wants to know what I ever went into the partnership for, anyway."

"I don't see why you ever did, myself," said
Roma, in a voice from the tombs.

The ironic twinkle in Baird's eyes became
more bright, and he stretched himself lazily, full
length, before the fire.

"I had a theory — have it still, for that matter
— that I ought to begin to be an active member of the community, — ought to have interests,
you know, occupations, that sort of thing. And
there was young Dumarais drudging along, and
no thanks from anybody. Seemed as little as I
could do, under the circumstances, to give him
a lift. Had to do something, you know, and
brokerage seemed rather less monotonous than
most mercantile pursuits. All that yelling and
clawing on 'Change, you know, and the uncertainty as to whom you're going to let into bank-
ruptcy next minute. Rather enlivening than
otherwise when you feel bored. Don't you think
so? I did."

Roma did not answer his question. He lay

looking up at her from beneath his quizzically
drooping eyelids, with his elbows on the ground
and his chin propped in his hands. And she
stared over his head, and said in a disagreeably
quiet voice: —

"Then all last winter, while you were visiting
me, you knew you were going to do this, and you
kept it from me."

"Jacques asked me not to mention it," explained Baird. "It was due him to keep it dark
till he was ready to announce it."

"And what was due to me?" she asked politely.

"Why, Roma! are you jealous?"

He leaned on one elbow and laid his other
hand on hers, which were clasped in her lap.

"It is not necessary to flatter yourself that
I am jealous," she replied calmly, and he with-
drew his hand. "It is ordinarily a matter of
indifference to me what confidences you share
with Mr. Dumarais and not with me; but in this
case I fail to understand how you justified to
yourself the right which you assumed of disposing
thus arbitrarily of my life even before you married me. One must expect to endure a certain
amount of tyranny at the hands of a husband,
even in these emancipated days, I suppose; but
most certainly before I married you, — before I
accepted you, — I had a right to be consulted on
matters relative to my future happiness. You

had no adequate excuse for imposing restrictions upon my life before my life was yours to order, and concealing these restrictions from me when you asked me to marry you."

"Disposing of your life! Restrictions!" said Curtis Baird, sitting up and staring at her. "That was the last thing I ever intended."

She continued to speak without noticing his interruption.

"I never hesitated to tell you how I hated New Orleans. You were quite aware of it. You even led me on sometimes to rail and deride. And all the while you were planning that I should live there."

He drew a sharp breath, and looked at her for a moment silently. Then he said: —

"It was stupid of me. But when I asked you to marry me, it did not occur to me that it made any difference whether we lived in New Orleans or Orange River Free State. Seemed only an external circumstance, after all. But I see, now, it was very stupid of me."

"If you had even told me when you asked me," she continued, with quiet bitterness, — "I had no right to know of your affairs before, but I did have then."

"Would you have refused me if you had known?" he asked.

And she said nothing.

"I am sorry I got you into this box," he re-

sumed presently. "I never meant to lead you
into the thing and not tell you how matters stood.
But a man can't always know just what he 'll do
when he 's in love. I meant to let you hear
about the business arrangement before I asked
you, but I lost my head that Sunday night.
And then — and then it did n't seem as if I
should have to stay there much of the time. I
thought I could go and come as I — as you
chose. I did n't know the thing was going to be
a hindrance in any way."

"Neither did I," she said, looking down and
speaking very low, very wearily.

He might have reproached her; he might have
told her he had given her a chance to withdraw
before it was too late, if she wished to do so,
but he could not say such things to her. He got
up and brought another log for the fire, and when
he sat down he said : —

"I did n't know Dumarais would make such
a point of my being on hand. I suppose he is
right. It 's no way to treat him, you know.
Makes the clerks respect the firm more, and
gives things a better look, to have me round.
Awful bore, but I 'm afraid we 've got to stand
it. I 'm sorry."

"I don't see why we 've got to stand it," said
Roma. "You don't need to keep up the partnership. If you want the excitement, I don't
see why you did n't go into business in Wall

Street. You can. It is n't necessary to stay down there."

Curtis Baird stroked his pointed beard.

"How about Jacques?" he said.

"I have been taking it for granted that you cared more for my comfort than for that of Mr. Dumarais," she said coolly. "Perhaps I made a mistake."

He pursed his lips and frowned as he shoved the fire closer together, saying: —

"I can't pension him off, you know; he 's not that kind. And if I 'm any sort of an honorable fellow I 've got to keep to the agreement till the year expires, at the least. No sufficient excuse for dissolving before then."

She looked indignant.

"And — and — you see, a man's got to have capital to run that kind of business; and if I leave Jacques in the lurch at the year's end, I 've — I 've just spoiled his prospects, that 's all. I 'd better have left him where he was. He could n't get in with his old firm again, and it would be an awful rub to have to go back to a salary."

"He found you; I don't see why he could n't find somebody else to go in with, just as well."

The twinkle had died out of Baird's eyes some time before, but now it came back for a moment as he said: —

"You don't find men like me every day in the

week, my dear.   I'm rather exceptional, on the whole."

But she refused to be amused.

"I don't see why, if it was capital he wanted, why he is n't contented with that, instead of taking your time, too."

"You see," Baird tried to explain, "we did n't arrange it that way.   I was hungering for occupation about that time, and he really does need me on hand sometimes.   I rather enjoy it, too.   I catch on to the accounts and the technique of the thing quite easily.   If only you were satisfied!"

"I am not satisfied," she said decisively.

"It was my fault in the very beginning," he acknowledged, "but I did not dream I should be restricted so."

"I know; you have told me that before," she answered.   "But you will not make the only reparation I ask you to make.   You will not give up the business."

He shook his head.

"I hate the place," she continued.   "You should have found out what was expected of you in the firm before you asked me.   You should not have taken so many things for granted."

She forgot that she, too, had taken one thing for granted, namely, that she could make him do as she pleased after she married him.

"I have been considerable of a fool," he said quietly.

He did not once reproach her for not confiding in him before she married him.

"But you will do nothing to remedy it?"

"No, dear; that is, not till Jacques is steady enough on his feet to stand alone, and that will take some time. He does n't speculate, and it 's uphill work saving money."

They arose and stood by the fire in silence a moment. Then she faced him, and her eyes flashed as she said sharply: —

"What is to be done about it?"

They looked at each other steadily without speaking, and read each other's thoughts and a certain disagreeable answer to that question.

"Except that it 's so horrid vulgar, you know," said Baird quietly.

She turned away from him, and went to one of the camps, and he followed, arranged a place for her on the spicy fir branches, tucked a blanket around her, and went out to the fire again.

As she lay under the open lean-to, she could see him sitting by the fire smoking a cigar. He stared into the flames solemnly; occasionally he stroked his beard with meditative deliberateness. Once he passed his hand through his hair with a weary gesture. She felt a lump in her throat when he did that, and she closed her eyes for a few minutes. When she opened them, he was sitting as before, staring through the fire.

It was his fault, she told herself. Yes, but

she had known, she had had time enough to withdraw, — she told herself that, too, for she was sincere. Why had n't she withdrawn? she asked herself half resentfully, half wonderingly, looking out at him. He was a handsome man. She liked his being so handsome. He was clever, also. More than once this summer she had felt proud to be his wife; it had been a new sensation to be proud because of her connection with some one else. And he had not uttered one word of reproach. Roma covered her face with the blanket.

Her eyes looked rather heavy when she came out later, but it was a very prickly blanket.

CHAPTER V

JOCELIN AND SYLVIA

AND down on the flat rock overhanging the valley Sylvia and Jocelin were watching the mist gather itself ghost-like out of the air just above the river and creep downward with the current. They did not speak for a long time. They watched the dark, shadowy mountains. They followed the river, here a gleam of silver, there a shroud of mist. The one light that twinkled in a hollow went out as they gazed. The smiling radiance of the intervale stretched across to the base of the mysterious shadows that stood uncertainly against the sky.

Sylvia seemed a part of the moonlight, a wraith-creature palely shining, very pure. She had never meant flesh and blood to Jocelin, as other women did. He almost wished this were not so — to-night. The light flashed into one of the rings she wore, a priceless, antique thing, dull Indian gold and a great flower of emerald-shavings set down into the gold, petalwise, about a rose diamond. It hung loose and heavy upon her slim hand. Jocelin thought of something his

mother had said once, — Mlle. Sylvia was rich.
He would have liked to be able to touch the delicate, gem-burdened hand, but — he did not want
to.

Jocelin was neither mercenary nor practical;
he was only pleasure-loving, and it gave him
more pleasure to feel the unapproachable chas-
tity, the separateness, of this woman than to
think of the delights he might purchase with her
millions. There were other women for other
uses. Jocelin had the sentimental reverence of
the unphilosophic sensualist for innocence. So
long as he could gratify his senses at other times,
why need he mar the spiritual harmony of this
unique experience? The knowledge that he was
wiser in sin than she, enhanced for him the exqui-
siteness of his self-fostered melancholy. Speaking to her of love would mean, if she responded,
bringing her to his level, — there was nothing
new, nothing piquante, in doing that. And, if
she did not respond, it would mean disaster, — no
more moon-maiden, untouched, unconscious, to be
worshiped.

But that remark of his mother's remained with
him. If he should succeed! She was very rich!
It would be comfortable to have money. Women
were women after all; and during the months of
his acquaintance with her, he had had a curious
feeling that the next time he saw her, the next
time he chose to look at her, he should desire

her. Perhaps the non-fulfillment of this prophetic
impression attracted him quite as much as her
innocence. He glanced at her, half-expectant of
a familiar sensation and stimulus, and this time
also she baffled him. Not a line, not a curve
of her, aroused unholy appetite. She sat very
still. Her eyes were luminous and thoughtful;
her face was pale, pure, and controlled. Would
it be worth while, would it be interesting, to try
to arouse her?

"Mademoiselle, you told me, before you went
away from the South, that you were going to ask
me to make you a promise."

"And you remembered it?" she said smiling.

"Yes, I remembered it. I do not forget the
things you say to me."

At the caress of his voice the heart - hunger
stirred within her, tempting her, and she moved
almost imperceptibly and looked at him.

"No, I do not forget, because— Will you
marry me?" he said.

One little sign from her, and he would touch
her. Did not his eyes say so? Very soft they
were, those eyes, and sad; the ecstasy of sadness
in their shining depths allured her. She thought
of his wretched young life, and the pathos of it
made her throat ache. What did it matter if he
had sinned? Whose fault was it that this was
so? Not his! Not his, with the sin-tainted eyes
confessing and unashamed, — not his, with the

seraph mouth and the seducer's smile! Would
he kiss her if she moved? If she might but
touch the brown throat, the soft, short hair!
Other women were given these joys. What was
sin? Could he help it? She loved him; what
did it matter what he had done? Who was she
that she should withhold herself from him? She
thought of his naïve confession, — "I have done
many wicked things; I have been very dissipated," — and its childlike frankness seemed to
divest his misdemeanors of their blackness. She
thought of those musing words: "It has always
seemed to me that it is presumptuous in me to
think that I could love a human being, a woman,
with the holiness, the unselfishness, that the word
' love ' means to me. Others claim that they do
it, but how can they hope to?"

If he could say this, if he could feel this with
the best of him, what did other things matter?
Other women gave themselves to men that they
loved. Why must she deny herself? He would
give her the caresses she might ask; his voice
said it, his eyes said it, his lips waited. One
little motion, Sylvia; will you make it? See!
his eyes are growing sure that you will.

He will give her what she asks, because she
loves him. Yes, she knows this. He will give
her her pleasure, and he will take his pleasure,
willingly, because she — loves him. He will
touch her; he will take her in his arms, here in

the moonlight on the mountain-top. Ah, the red mouth trembling! His eyes are very certain of what she will do. Too certain, Jocelin; it was not wise.

His red mouth will burn upon her lips, kissing her. Why will he kiss her if he does not love her?

Yes, Sylvia, answer the question to your heart, and then — show us how low you intend to fall.

How does she know he does not love her? She knows! Any woman would know. If he did love her, would there be sin black enough to keep them apart? How could there be? Is she willing that he should kiss her? Is she willing that he should take her in his arms, not loving her? There are women — who would be willing. What are such women called? Is it to be as low as that, Sylvia, — because you love him?

He is waiting. Look into his eyes! He is very sure of what you will do. Will you?

"Sit farther off," said Sylvia. "I have something to say to you."

He bent his head and drew himself away, almost to her feet. Decidedly, he had aroused her! And the result was to be more interesting than he had supposed.

"O voice, O music! do not be a lost soul!" she said, and her own voice was full of the soft, sighing quality of the night wind.

"Go apart from me and make ready our defense against the coming of the Judgment Day. Speak for me! How shall I have need to speak after the Divine Pity has heard the music of your pleading? Tell Him, the Judge, that you have tempted me, — that it is accomplished. He will know if I have fallen. I do not know. Tell Him I have gone through the remainder of my life with the taint upon me, rejoicing, not that I have overcome the temptation, but that I have known what it is to desire the things of the flesh. Tell Him I have forsaken irresolution and tasted of the fruit of the Tree of Knowledge. That which is evil I have looked upon, knowing its name, and henceforth I choose the good. These things you are to tell Him, defending me, and then the terrible thing at the end. Tell Him — I do not repent. Ask Him if I must. He will know. Do not lie there with your face against the rock and moan; there is no need of your remorse. I am nearer salvation because of you. But I do not want to repent. It is the taint that is upon me, and perhaps that brings salvation, — I do not know."

She looked down at him as he lay crouched upon the rock, his face hidden against her dress; and when she spoke again, there was an added tenderness in her words: —

"But it is not alone for me that you shall plead when the Day comes, O tired voice, all worn and

wasted here on earth! What will it matter when
we are in heaven and your spirit sings?"

He moved, and she added hurriedly: —

"Take away your lips from the hem of my
gown!" Then, touched by his obedience: —

"If it comforts you to know it, I grieve, too.
But now you are to go away from me. You
have well-nigh destroyed your earthly voice; it
is time to build a heavenly one in your soul. It
has come to me that Jeanne will teach you.
That was why she was taken away so young, so
lovely, with all her world before her."

Sylvia was explaining gently, as if to a child.

"God took her away to give you something to
do, and to save your soul alive. It is not very
glorious, the writing of little fragile songs that
some one else has made. But, alas! I do not
think that you are fit for anything glorious now.
All Jeanne's music that she used to make has
gone to heaven with her, and we on earth cannot do without that music. Bring it back to us!
It is not your name that God means shall be
famous; it is Jeanne's. This is the promise you
are to make me: You are to save your voice, that
you may sing Jeanne's songs; to keep your head
clear and your hand steady, that you may write
Jeanne's music. For Jeanne's sake, and the
world's sake, — and mine — mine! If the great
multitude stands before the throne of the Lamb,
singing praise night and day, and your voice is

not there, I do not think God will call that place
heaven. And if I die, and enter into a darkness
full of groans and terrible cries, and still I hear
you, I shall not be in hell. And I shall be ac-
cursed!"

She stopped with a gasp, as if she found herself saying more than she had intended to say.

Jocelin shivered convulsively, and began to
sob in an hysterical fashion, unrestrainedly, as
a woman might have done. He clung to her
gown and pressed it to his lips. Sylvia pulled
the skirt away, almost roughly, and stood up on
the rock out of his reach, and, as the low, smothered sound of his weeping continued, she turned
her back upon where he lay, and flung up her
arms with a gesture of despair. Even a spiritual
union with him seemed a little flat just then.

She looked out upon the moonlit valley, her
exaltation gone, a sense of chill and disappointment, even of disgust, at her heart. And all
this because her own words had made him weep.
If Sylvia herself had been endowed with fewer
hysterical possibilities, or less self-control, she
might not have felt the disgrace of his tears so
keenly.

"Do not be a lost soul!" she said wearily.
"Do not be a lost soul!"

She could think of nothing else to say, and
something in her tone — it may have been indifference — checked his crying. He raised him-

self, and saw her standing with her back to him, and his face grew a dull red.

Jocelin was neither intellectual nor spiritual, but he was sensitive, and he had an instinct for the dramatic fitness of things. That was why, at the present crisis, he did not speak; he only waited, kneeling on the rock, looking towards her, with shame and terror and self-loathing in his eyes, until she, becoming conscious of the stillness, turned and saw him.

"Ah! I hate, hate, hate myself!" he whispered fiercely.

She waited, saying nothing.

"I promise!" he said, and groaned, and hid his face in his hands.

Her pity awoke then, with a little of her love, and she said: —

"Sing to me, that I may carry away the memory of your voice, — your voice alone, the God-given part of you. Sing, for I do not want to remember other things."

And again he sang the one hundred and twenty-first psalm. But this time there was no humor in the situation.

CHAPTER VI

"I SAY, you people, look at that moon!"

The voice was that of Jacques, uplifted from a vantage-point above the camp, whither he and Enid had wandered.

"By Jove! So it is!" said Curtis Baird, and he dusted the cigar-ashes off the front of his flannel shirt. "Roma!"

Roma came out from beneath the lean-to with very tired eyes. Her husband glanced at her, took down a blanket that hung in the camp, and saying, "This is the way we do it!" proceeded to wrap it around her lengthwise, Indian fashion.

"Now crawl up behind the other lean-to! They're up there, and it's a good, open-sky sort of place. I'll bring a blanket for Miss Enid presently. Not cold, are you?"

"No."

She liked being taken care of. She liked his being such a gentleman. And she had said such horrid things to him!

She found Jacques and Enid sitting on the

rock above, discussing the moon, which hung in the sky like a bitten cracker.

"Jocelin! Jocelin!" called Baird, "bring Miss Sylvia up on top. We want you to sing ' See the Pale Moon ' It's worth seeing."

And finally the six were gathered together on the rocks, with the wide sky stretching above and around, and the mutilated moon shedding its slowly diminishing brightness upon them.

They all munched crackers and drank coffee. No, not all, for Enid was a homœopathist and did not approve of coffee. Jacques had tried to convert her to an appreciation of its merits the winter before, but had failed.

"Why is it that we never have a total eclipse of the moon except when the moon is full? I suppose I learned why once, but I've forgotten," said Enid.

"Because that's the only time the moon is all on hand," volunteered Jacques.

Baird laughed. "I think it is this way," he said, and proceeded to explain the theory by means of large and small crackers, and a tin cup for purposes of eclipse.

His wife watched him silently, comparing him with the other two men. He had not the practical business ability of Jacques, nor the artistic power of Jocelin, but he had more culture than either of them. She remembered how well he had known all the little plants and fungi along

the path as they came up the mountain; how he
had spied tiny, woodsy things that none of the
others had had eyes to see until he pointed them
out. She remembered how he had told her of
spending whole days alone in these woods, among
these mountains. Alone! It implied a certain
purity of soul in him which startled her. She
looked at him as he revolved his crackers, that
whimsical smile upon his lips, the wayward twinkle in his eyes. She thought he looked tired,
but the others did not seem to notice it. She
found herself ruminating upon the idea that he
was pleasanter to live with than either of the
other men.

He finished his explanation and ate the crackers as an illustration of the ultimate redistribu-
tion of matter in the universe. He was so clever!
Clever in a way that Jacques and Jocelin could
never be. He had a background of general information and general scholarship to draw from,
and they had not.

"What good does it do you?" inquired Jacques
curiously.

"What?" asked Baird.

"Why, all these tail-ends of wisdom you cram
into that noddle of yours?"

Baird laughed. "We can't all be specialists,
you know," he answered. "It does me good; it
entertains me. I'm made so that I need a lot of
entertaining to make existence worth while."

"Are n't you fond of any one thing more than another, Mr. Baird?" asked Enid. "Are they all equally pleasant to you?"

"N-n-o!" he said slowly; "I can't say that they are."

"So he has a preference, a specialty, after all!" cried Jacques. "Out with it! What is it you 're fondest of? Not cotton brokerage, I know."

"I beg to be excused," smiled Baird. "Not that I mind unfolding my soul to such a sympathetic audience. But my wife is present. She might feel embarrassed at having her name brought into the conversation, you know."

It was a pretty compliment; Roma liked it. She sat in the shadow behind Enid and Sylvia. The three women had drawn together and the men were facing them. Roma felt herself blushing in the shadow, and realized that to her it was odd to blush at compliments from her own husband.

"Talking about specialties," said Jacques, "I 've decided to go home to-morrow."

"Better start now, then," said Baird; "train leaves at quarter after eight in the morning. If you go now," he looked at his watch, "you can take it leisurely through the woods. Rather dark, but if you must!"

"I take the afternoon train," laughed Jacques. "No joking. I 've got to."

"Rather sudden, is n't it?"

"Yes," Jacques acknowledged. "But I've been thinking it over, and it is best all round."

"I will go with you," said Jocelin.

"Hullo!" ejaculated Baird. "You've no pressing engagements, young man?"

"No, but it may be as well for me to be on the scene of action early."

"Noble sentiment!" This from Baird.

"I suppose I can depend on you for the first?" Jacques continued to his partner.

"First of what? — January?"

"No, October." Jacques said this in his business tone.

"Suppose we say the fifteenth?" suggested Baird with teasing blandness.

"The fifteenth, then, of October."

"And if it comes on a Sunday?" murmured the incorrigible Baird.

"The fifteenth of October," repeated Jacques.

"Wouldn't Mr. Baird be just as useful if he attended to the business in New York?" inquired Roma, speaking from the shadow.

"No, madame," said Jacques. "Candor obliges me to confess that he would not."

"October is so early, Mr. Dumarais! People always lose the effect of their summer if they go home as early as that. And Curtis is not acclimated."

Curtis smiled.

"I wouldn't be anxious about him," observed

Jacques; "he's tougher than you think. It won't do him a bit of harm to come home then. If he has tried to make you believe he's delicate, Mrs. Baird, don't you believe him; he's only putting on, and trying to get you to plead for him, so he can stay up here and see the leaves turn red. He's seen them do it for some thirty odd years. Just don't you encourage him in his idle ways, Mrs. Baird."

It is always nettling to be instructed by an outsider in the manners and foibles of one's parents, or children, or — husband (even when one has been married to that husband but two months, and has never acknowledged to any particularly deep affection for him).

"It is I who do not want to go home," said Roma. "Mr. Baird says he must, because it is not fair to leave you down there."

"And you would save him from rushing into the jaws of death and dengué fever. Ah, yes, madame! I understand. Baird, you're a lucky fellow."

"I am afraid it is simply because I do not want to go," persisted Roma.

"And he is such a brute, he says if he goes, you must!" added Jacques. "Baird, I wouldn't have believed it of you."

"He's not a brute at all!" said Roma, impatiently, and they all laughed, — except her husband, who smiled in his own inscrutable fashion.

"I hasten to withdraw all explanations and assertions. I am not in this thing. I will retire gracefully while there is yet time," said Jacques. "Let us look at the moon."

It was almost covered by this time, and they watched in silence until the shadow had crept over the last bright bit of the edge, and the little planet hung above them like a dull, brown-skinned orange. The shadow had brought out the solidity of the moon in a curious manner. It was no longer a flat disk; it was a globe, small, and rounded out in the heavens. The blue-black sky was alive with stars, depths upon depths of stars. This was the month for meteors, and now and again a falling star would trail across the twinkling darkness, appearing out of space and vanishing into it again.

"Who made a wish that last time?" asked Roma.

"I did," said Jacques, and he looked at Enid.

"There goes another!" cried Roma, "but that was too quick. I wonder what we all wished. Would n't it be entertaining to know?"

"I am perfectly willing to tell mine," said Enid.

"It would destroy the charm if we told," interrupted Sylvia hastily.

"I 'll bet I can guess what Mrs. Baird wished," said Jacques.

"What?" demanded Roma.

"That you would n't have to go home in October."

"I did n't wish that at all."

"Then there is something you wish for more than staying away from New Orleans?" said Baird.

"Yes."

"Are you going to tell him, Mrs. Baird?" teased Jacques. "Wives always tell their husbands everything, don't they?"

"That depends upon the husbands," Roma answered.

"Bravo!" cried Jacques; "there speaks the modern woman."

"That is n't modern," declared Enid. "It was just as much a fact before the flood as it is now."

"I don't believe it was acknowledged so boldly," Jacques insisted.

"Perhaps not."

"You don't mean to say you 're trying to reduce the modern woman to a definition, Jacques?" Baird asked the question.

"With three to study, one might hope to get at a little of the truth." As Jacques said this, he faced about and stared at the three women with uncompromising directness.

"We might make a new game," suggested Baird, "and call it 'The Modern Woman, a Characteristic Game.'"

"Capital!" cried Jacques. "We might invent the characteristics now. Each man write three, mix them up, and guess who wrote them."

"We shall do the guessing," said Roma. "If you make game of us, we shall claim equal rights and make game of you."

"There's one of her characteristics to start on!" said Jacques.

The moon was beginning to come out of the shadow. There was a scribbling of lead-pencils upon the backs of envelopes, while the three women, huddled together, conversed in whispers.

"It is strange!" said Roma; "one is so far away from people! It makes the trees and the rocks seem full of life, as if they were human beings. I feel as if I were on another planet when I look down upon that wide valley full of mist."

Sylvia murmured something from Shelley, about tall peaks islanded with mist.

"Let us slip away soon; I want to tell you something," whispered Enid.

"Not now," Sylvia answered.

The pencils ceased, and Jacques struck a match in order to see if what he had written was legible. Baird then shuffled the papers, and, by the aid of several matches, read them aloud.

"She is determined upon having her own way."

"Mr. Dumarais wrote that one," said Enid promptly.

"And why do you think so?" demanded Jacques.

"Because you are so bent on having your own way yourself."

"Rule that one out!" Roma cried. "It is a masculine characteristic."

"Let's compromise and call it a common attribute," suggested Baird.

"I call it a victory for our side," declared Enid.

Jacques groaned.

"She possesses that generosity of mind which has hitherto been accorded to men alone. She is equally large-minded and fair when she is in the right as when she is in the wrong."

Roma started.

"Well?" said her husband.

"Nothing."

"Oh, I thought you were going to guess."

"Nobody ready?" asked Jacques.

"I'm not certain," said Enid; and Sylvia added, "Nor I, but it argues a generous mind on the part of the writer."

"We might save that one, and come back to it. Here's another: 'It is not of herself that she thinks; she strives that others may be saved.'"

"Is that Mr. Castaigne?" inquired Sylvia gently.

"Right! Jocelin, if that characteristic is a

reflection of your own mind, Miss Sylvia has paid you a very pretty compliment. You 'd better get up and make a bow."

"I do," said Jocelin, and as he stood up he looked off towards the north.

"Tell me, is it the beginning of the dawn I see? — that whiteness?"

"Perhaps. It does begin pretty far round sometimes, but it 's rather early now. Let me see!"

Curtis Baird stood up beside Jocelin and looked for some seconds in silence towards the place Jocelin indicated. Then he said, in a quiet voice: —

"It is the Northern Lights."

The others scrambled hastily to their feet.

The faint whiteness in the north was growing definite; it gleamed, it moved. Gradually an arc of light came out against the sky, and along the arc, from left to right, the pale-green luminous shadows began to dance. Up and up they mounted, now great sweeps of light, now pointed, knife-like shafts, now fading fan-rays. There was no color save the pale green that was almost white. There was no sound, save once or twice a faint crackle in the air. The procession of shining ghosts grew taller and taller as it moved along the arc. After a while the pageant faded, as a rainbow fades, mistily, slowly, imperceptibly. Those who had watched it spoke in hushed voices, and went down softly to the camp. The eclipse was almost over.

"We shall have a couple of hours for sleep before the dawn begins," said Curtis Baird; "I should advise you to embrace the opportunity if you can."

CHAPTER VII

THE DAWN

SYLVIA lay very still under the lean-to, but she was not asleep. She knew that Enid, beside her, was awake, and she had caught a blink of Roma's eyelids from the farther corner of the little shed. Enid had tried to draw Sylvia away to a quiet place where they could be alone together and talk, but Sylvia was white and quiet and unresponsive, and Enid's habit of considering her friend's welfare made her suppress her own longing for sympathy, and lie down in patient silence upon the sweet pine branches.

Sylvia' could look out and see Jacques and Curtis Baird and Jocelin lying about the camp in picturesque and unconventional attitudes, — Jacques, under the other lean-to, changing his position restlessly every few minutes, but always keeping his back turned resolutely to the fire; Curtis Baird, stretched full length on the ground and propped on one elbow, his chin in his hand, staring into the flames — once or twice he got up softly and put a log on the fire; Jocelin, half sitting, half lying, against a blanketed rock — asleep. Yes, Jocelin was asleep.

After a long while Sylvia crept slowly and
softly away from Enid's side, and stood up in
the open space by the fire. Enid watched her
go, and moved slightly, but Sylvia did not turn.
And Enid did not follow her.

"You will hear the birds better if you go over
on the wilderness side," whispered Curtis Baird.

But Sylvia shook her head. As she tiptoed
past Jocelin he opened his eyes and smiled, and
fell asleep again. And she went on down to the
ledge where he and she had sat in the moonlight.
The place was full of her words and his sobs.

The color was beginning to creep back into the
trees. The river and all the valley lay hidden
asleep beneath the mist. The moon, of palest
silver, fading white, looked across to the east
where the sky flushed faintly pink. It was a
weary moon. The leaves on the young poplar-
trees beneath the ledge were absolutely still. Now
and again the flute-notes of a thrush came out of
the silence and melted back to it. The dawn
languor pressed at the heart of life, and the
pulse-beats of the world were weak and slow.

Sylvia stared down at the wide mist-river.

"Is it that I do not love him any more?" she
asked herself wearily. "No, — oh, no! I want
to love him. Jocelin!"

She lay down on the rock and looked sidewise
over the valley. The mist was turning rosy. She
watched it idly. Her exhaustion was too great

for tears. No, let Jocelin cry like a sick woman if he chose!

"O voice! I wish that you and I were dead!" she whispered. Her mouth trembled dejectedly.

"There will never be any one like that again. 'I will lift up mine eyes unto the hills from whence cometh my help.'"

She looked across to the great mountains coming back, pale icy blue in the dawn-light, and for a long time she was so still she seemed to lie asleep, — all but her eyes, which were fixed wide open quietly.

Her spirit had been shaken to its depths that night by the violence of unusual emotions and the swiftness of their transitions. A great temptation, a great exaltation, and a great disgust! Despite her inherited moral asceticism, her pampered, self-conscious apathy, her hysteria, secretly indulged but unmistakable, these experiences were possible to Sylvia. What was it she had felt when she saw him lying there shaken with sobs? Disgust? Was it? Why not sympathy? Who should have understood his weakness if not she?

When he gave the promise, impelled by her insistent silence, and when he sang, kneeling on the rock with the shadow of despair still in his eyes, her love began to come back faintly; and in after years that love, fed by her pity, transfigured by her gratitude, became a religion with her.

But it is to be doubted whether, all her life long, she ever forgave Jocelin those tears. She had shunned the memory of them persistently throughout the night, and now, at the beginning of the new day, she was deliberately thrusting them from her mind, in order to think the best of him. Sylvia was very proud. Perhaps she did not care to remember that the man whom she had loved, and whom she still wanted to love, was so degenerate.

He had promised! And he had prayed for help!

She watched the mist, and let that thought sink into her soul, strengthening her. She had fretted in self-distrust; she had wasted her life in wailing over her own uselessness, and, behold! God had given her a great gift. It seemed she was to save a human soul. Through her will Jocelin had made this promise. What did it matter if she had not human happiness, so Jocelin had life, and through her? It was enough to be delivered from herself and to deliver him. And while she waited the long, long years, ah! idleness would be unbearable! She must work now. Working meant writing to Sylvia. Writing what? . . .

That was the way the inspiration came to her, born with the beginning of the new day. Very still she lay, wide-eyed, but the pink color of the dawn fluttered in her cheeks.

Sylvia's great-grandfather wrote a play once, — to his undoing, — and her grandfather prayed prayers that were poems. Doubtless all this had something to do with the book that Sylvia wrote. All Jocelin's little foibles went into the book, his weaknesses, his sins. The good and the evil of him were set down with a curious dispassionateness, considering that it was Sylvia who wrote the book. It may be that, after all, her love for him had been mainly a matter of imagination. Imagination was always the strongest quality Sylvia possessed. Or it may be that, unconsciously, she did not forgive.

What help did the hills bring, Sylvia? What did the mountains say to you, that you should smile as you looked out over the valley? Was it the glow of the mist reflected in your eyes, that kindled them?

The mist? What was the matter with the mist? Something was happening to it. It was coming up swiftly, in a mass, all pink. Flying up! There was no escaping it.

Sylvia clung to the moss, awe-stricken, and the pink cloud came up from the valley and shut out all the world, and made a rosy light everywhere, and no other thing.

She heard Enid's voice calling her from a distance: "Sylvia! Sylvia!"

But she did not answer. She sat still in the midst of the cloud, and she thought: —

"Is it outside of me, or is it in my soul, this rosy light?"

But presently she became aware of voices. Some one quite near her gasped and said: —

"Curtis!"

There were hasty footsteps, and Curtis Baird said: —

"Ah! here you are!"

The first voice gasped again, and Baird murmured: —

"Why! why!" in a pleased tone. "Frightened?"

"What is it, Curtis?"

"The mist has come up suddenly, because of some shifting of the air-currents, and a sudden change in the temperature. It is unusual, but there's nothing to be alarmed about in it. It's perfectly explainable according to the laws of physics."

There was a short pause, and he continued: —

"Look up, dear! It is a lovely light."

"How did you know where I was?"

"Oh, I had my eye on you when you left the camp. Did n't you call me?"

"Yes! I — I was startled."

"Don't move, if you 're comfortable."

"I — I" — Such a tearful, muffled voice!

"There, there, dear! It has been too much for you. I ought not to have sprung an all-night affair like this on you so soon, when you are n't

used to the woods and the outdoor life. It has
been too exciting. Don't cry! The dawn's always a nasty time, anyway. Everything's below
par then, you know. Don't cry! We'll have
some hot coffee when this mist blows off, and
you'll feel better."

"It isn't that," said the muffled voice; "it
isn't that at all! I'm going South with you."

"No, no!" he answered. "That's all right!
I've thought about it. You needn't, you know.
You can stay here, and give your two sisters a
winter in New York, and I'll run up, say once a
month, for a few days. How's that? It's only
fair, since I got you into the scrape, that I should
suf — that I should do what I can to make life en-
durable to you. Don't worry about going South."

"I'm not. I've changed my mind. I want
to go. I" —

Sylvia heard only incoherent murmurs and
protests after that. Jocelin could never have
kissed her as Curtis Baird kissed his wife. The
thought stung her. Other women could be happy.
And the look in Jocelin's eyes when he had asked
her to marry him came back to her, and brought
the sense of shame, of taint. She should never
marry Jocelin, she should never marry any one,
because some one — was it he or she? — had dese-
crated the sacrament.

The mist sank on a sudden, as swiftly as it
had risen, and began to waste away in the valley.

Roma and her husband were behind a neighboring rock, and as they got up to go back to the camp, Roma said : —

"The fifteenth of October does come on Sunday."

Some of the far mountains had caught the sunlight, and there was a patch of brightness on the poplar-trees, but the beech-wood and the pines below were still in shadow, and ragged patches of mist frayed out among the treetops.

The exultation which accompanies an act of creation had given place to sickening weariness. Sylvia came into the camp looking white and almost stern.

"We were about to send out a search party," said Baird. "Miss Enid felt convinced that you had fallen over a precipice."

She warmed her hands at the embers of the dying fire, over which Roma was toasting bread. Jocelin came to her, and bent down to warm his hands, also.

"When I awoke in that shining mist, I thought that I was dead and heaven had come, and I waited for your face," he said.

She did not answer him, she did not look up, but she put her hand inadvertently into a little flame that woke up out of the embers.

Jacques was ruefully trying to straighten the coffee-pot, upon which he had unwittingly trampled during the mist.

Enid sat by the lean-to, pretending to eat a piece of toast. Sylvia went over to her, realizing suddenly that she and Enid had said little to each other that night.

"I have thought of a story," she said softly, "and I must write it. We shall go down and work. I am impatient to begin. I shall work all the rest of my life, and never, never stop. We shall be very busy, Enid! Let us go down. I think I shall never leave anything unfinished again."

After all, was Jocelin's soul to be the only one saved?

CHAPTER VIII

JOCELIN GOES FORTH TO CONQUER

IN the early morning, when all the green things in the woods were still dew-drenched and drooping sleepily, the campers straggled down the mountain-side.

Jocelin went first, singing.

It was a wonderful thing to hear Jocelin's sweet voice, so clear and joyous, in the midst of the newly wakened woods. Jocelin sang only glad songs that morning. So lightly he trod the mountain path, he seemed not to feel the earth under his feet. He held his head triumphantly, singing straight before him with rapt gaze, and the melancholy cry in his voice was as the beatific sadness of a purified and pardoned spirit. He sang the happy little songs Jeanne used to make and sing, — the love-songs, the tender lullabies, the bits of prayer. He spoke to no one, and he did not look behind.

"It is like having little Jeanne with us again," said Roma.

Curtis Baird and Roma came after Jocelin, walking together and saying little, — if words count for much.

Enid and Sylvia followed, hand in hand, and for a while they, too, were silent. Enid was thinking of the winter that was coming, and the work that was to be her life. Sylvia was listening to Jocelin, and giving thanks to God for His blessings. Over and over she said to herself: —

"Jocelin has promised! It is I who have been allowed to save him."

And the joy in her heart was strength. Sylvia, also, was beginning to live.

Jacques came at the end of the little procession, switching the drops off the wet bushes that leaned into the path. Sometimes, when he looked at Enid, his keen eyes softened; but sometimes, too, his chin grew more square, his mouth more firm, the pose of his head more military and obstinate.

"I believe that fellow is going to amount to something, after all," said Curtis Baird, nodding towards Jocelin. "What a blessing it is for me that I was born with money! Think what I might have come to!"

"You would not have been like him," asserted his wife.

Baird smiled as if her remark pleased him, but persisted teasingly: —

"No-o! I have n't his heavenly voice, you know."

Jocelin began to sing the little song of spring, only one line, then he broke off short and was silent a while.   Truly Jeanne walked with them down the mountain-side that morning.

When Jocelin began again, he chose the "Marseillaise."   Jacques involuntarily followed suit, and stopped abruptly after the first three bars. Curtis Baird hummed the air absent-mindedly for a moment, but his voice soon died away, and he trudged along at his wife's side, his chin sunk upon his chest, his eyes fixed thoughtfully on the ground.   Enid came back from her dreams of social reform to the memory of Mardi Gras night. They all walked on abstractedly, seeing visions: —

A long table and a blazing bowl in the centre, and behind the colored flames a face with parted lips, singing.

Whose was that vision?

"I have made love to your — women, and they have found me — not altogether — unpleasing. I — speak for one of them."

Who remembered that?   Was it a pleasant memory?

They sang the song loudly, merrily, around the table.

"Your friend is sensitive, — Jocelin is lovable, — pardon me! "

Those were biting memories.

Jocelin sang on alone to the end.   When he stopped, his companions awoke once more to the wet, green woods, and the beech-trees with the sunshine up in the tops of them, and morning twilight underneath.

When they rested by the brook, they talked together of the coming winter and their work. It was an inspiration to hear Jocelin tell of his plans, — the very tone of his voice bespoke consecration. He had never before been so humble-minded, — so full of hope and energy. Even Jacques, in whom long experience of the enthusiasms of his step-brother had engendered skepticism, unbent and grew almost sympathetic. He thought perhaps Jocelin really did feel more responsibility about succeeding, for his mother's sake, now that he was all she had left. And without doubt this mountain air had done him good, for his voice was stronger than it had been in years.

Sylvia was the only one who did not talk of what she meant to do; and the others, except Enid, did not notice then, because they had never thought of Sylvia in connection with anything active. She was only rich and delicate. But they remembered it afterwards, when Sylvia's book came out. They remembered, too, how much Jocelin had talked.

When they came out of the woods into the long pasture behind the lodge, the valley had caught the sunlight, and the great mountains smiled upon Jocelin.

Was it to be success with him? Was there some one who should save him from himself, after all?

Bravo, Jocelin!

BOOK IV

"MAN, OH, NOT MEN!"

"Man, oh, not men! A chain of linkèd thought,
Of love and might to be divided not."
                    PERCY BYSSHE SHELLEY.

CHAPTER I

MONSIEUR ADVISES

MONSIEUR DUMARAIS sat in his little book-room with a tiny volume of Daudet in his hand. The old house was very quiet, but monsieur had grown used to that since Jeanne had died and Jocelin had gone away. The piano was never touched now, and no busy, hurrying little feet ran up and down the galleries. Madame's slow, weighty tread and the occasional slipshod patter of a servant were the only sounds of motion through the house all day, until Jacques' brisk, firm step was heard upon the stairs at six o'clock. Monsieur began to watch for that step in the middle of the afternoon. There was always a possibility that Jacques might come home before six, you know.

He was watching now, in the dark, silent house. Madame had gone to the French Opera matinée. Jacques tormented her into going occasionally; he told her it cheered her up. She sometimes came home and shed tears, because the singing made her think of Jocelin; but Jacques found that most things made her think of Jocelin, and concluded that it was better for her to be reminded of Jocelin's singing than of his other characteristics.

The early December darkness was already gathering in the corners of the little room. The day was bleak, and madame had had a fire made in the grate before she went out, but it had died down to embers, and the maid had forgotten to attend to it.

That was Jacques' step, after all! And it could not be more than half past four. Monsieur found himself astonished against his will. Something must have happened.

"Where is that Aurelia-Josephine-Stéphanie-Maria? Why does n't she keep this fire going?" said Jacques. "Where is maman?"

"This last one is Stéphanie," replied monsieur. "I heard her talking to the milkman in the alley not long ago. Your maman has gone to the matinée."

"Of course! I forgot!"

Jacques put some coal on the fire, sat down, and drummed his hands on his knees.

"You are at home early, my son."

"John Harris came into the office to-day," Jacques began, with his usual lack of preamble. "He has just come from New York. He met Jocelin on the street there."

"Ah?"

Monsieur had felt convinced that something

disagreeable was to happen when he heard Jacques on the stairs.

"Jocelin borrowed a quarter from him."

The silence which followed this statement condemned Jocelin more severely than words could have done.

"He did not tell me that at first. He asked me if I knew how wretchedly Jocelin was looking, and I said no, he had not sent us his photograph lately. He told me Jocelin asked about New Orleans, and wept when he spoke of his mother. Harris is a good sort. He said, 'I know geniuses are a trial to the flesh of us ordinary mortals in most cases, and I guess your step-brother is no exception to the general rule; but I thought that — well — for his mother's sake you might like to know how matters stood with him. I gathered from his remarks that he had not kept you thoroughly informed.' And then he eyed me for a second and blurted out, ' Tell you what, Dumarais, that fellow 's in an awful bad way. Looks as if he 'd die any minute.' "

After a pause Jacques continued : —

"I suppose I shall have to hunt him up and bring him home."

"Did this young man know his address?" asked Monsieur Dumarais.

"No. Maman sends to the general post-office."

"If I had known what I was bringing upon you, I should never have married," said monsieur.

"Ah, bah!" said Jacques.

"When your mother hears this, it will make her ill."

"There is no need that she should hear it. I shall say I am going North, and while there I shall look up Jocelin. When I am there, I can write that he is coming home with me for a vacation."

"Oh, my son, you are a very good son to me and to her."

"Why not?" said Jacques.

"You will have some difficulty in finding him."

"Perhaps. I shall go to his last address, — that was eight months ago, is it not? Harris saw him in some little street off the Bowery. I can always apply to the police. Perhaps he will be dead in the mean while."

There was a hopeful inflection in Jacques' voice as he suggested this possibility, but he was not hard-hearted, he was only extremely upright. After a moment he added: —

"A quarter! If it had been twenty-five dollars, I should not have cared."

He crossed the little room, took down a book, put it up again, walked back to the fire, and stood by the mantel-piece, shoving the toe of his boot between the bars of the grate.

"There was no more bad news?"

"No. It is to be hoped that Providence will consider that sufficient for one twenty-four hours."

"You leave soon?"

"I think so. In a day or two. I must see maman about my trunk."

"Your mother has gone to Madame Chassard's after the matinée."

Jacques laughed.

"We shall have more of the charms of Mademoiselle Félicie for dinner in that case. Truly, I am a heavy responsibility to maman. It requires great agility to elude her attempts to make me a married man. Ha, ha! She is a nice little girl, Mademoiselle Félicie, but maman will have to comprehend that we do not conduct our affairs as they did when she was young. I refuse distinctly to be proposed for."

"You are right; she is a nice little girl, that Mademoiselle Félicie," observed Monsieur Dumarais with peculiar quietness. "She reminds me of Jeanne. Of course she is not gifted, she does not sing, but, on the whole, that would be too painful. In some ways I believe she is more efficient than our Jeanne. Ah, that dear child! I do not cease missing her."

"Nor I," said Jacques, glancing uneasily at his father. "Nor I."

The delinquent Stéphanie came down the hall, glanced in at the door with a perturbed countenance, and, seeing the ruddy fire and also the young master of the house, fled before a rebuke could be administered.

"That girl is no good," said Jacques.

"I know, my son; but your mother at her age begins to find the housekeeping more of a burden. She can no longer maintain the same rigor with these creatures that she used to. They take advantage. It needs a younger woman."

There was another silence which Jacques tried not to find significant.

"I think, while I am in the North, I will run up to Boston, and call on Miss Sylvia and Miss Enid," he remarked presently in a low voice. "I told them they might expect to see me again in about a year."

Monsieur arose, and came and stood beside his son, laying his hand upon the young man's shoulder. For a long time the two remained thus, without speaking, but at last Jacques said in the same low voice:—

"Well, my father?"

"Perhaps I should say nothing, my son; it is not necessary that you should listen, however."

"Oh, no! I shall be glad to hear," Jacques answered, but his tone was listless.

"Why is it that you set your heart upon the impossible woman, Jacques? She is of the race of Jeanne d'Arc, this Northern girl, in her voice, her bearing, her beliefs. That kind is not to be possessed by one man; she belongs to a cause, to the people. If one insists upon falling in love with such women, one must be content to assume towards them the attitude of a Dante; they will not permit any other. Fortunately, they are the exceptions."

"Not as much as you think. There are dozens of them in the North. She told me so herself. They are increasing every day," said Jacques moodily.

"Perhaps! perhaps!" said monsieur, soothingly. "Of course I do not go out; I do not see the world. But there!"—with a comprehensive gesture towards his beloved book-shelves —"there you do not find the Frenchman telling you that Jeanne d'Arc is the general type. And the Frenchman knows his world and his women."

"Ah, France! that is different," said Jacques. "But France is not the world. Of course the Frenchwomen are not like that, with their education."

"Nor the New Orleans women," added his father.

"Nor the New Orleans women," Jacques assented. "But neither are they all the world."

"But she would be obliged to live here, my son. I tell you I am right. It may be, as you say, that all the women are beginning to be exceptions to the rule; I do not know. But of this I am sure, that this one woman could never come here and keep this house, and mend your clothes, and bring your children into the world.

"No! She would die, or the house would explode. I am more inclined to think that it is the house which would explode. If I speak with force, it is because I wish to see you happy. I say again, such women are not to be married. Worship them, yes! Adore them! And when you do marry, you will love your wife the more tenderly, and be a better husband to her, because you have endured the discipline of a purely ideal and spiritual emotion. Understand me, my son! She is adorable, that woman. I do not say that there are women more worthy to be loved than she, but I say there are women who will make better wives. And one does not need to go North to seek them; there are many here."

"Oh, hordes of them!" cried Jacques. "Maman discovers at least two or three new ones every week, and Mrs. Baird introduced me to six in one evening, when she gave her *bal poudré*."

"I repeat, they are to be worshiped, the great, the universal women, but that is a different affair from a wife. It is not the same kind of affection."

"I have not said that I should marry anybody," said Jacques, "or worship her either. And here is maman. It will be just as well to change the subject."

Madame entered, puffing slightly.

"You home, Jacques? But it is not as late as that, no?"

"I am going to New York the day after tomorrow," said Jacques.

"Then you will surely find Jocelin?"

Madame sat down in a chair and began to cry, and to talk English. She had lately conceived the idea that Jacques was more easily persuaded by English than by French.

"It is now eight monsse an ee will naut say nossing of wat ee do. Ma po' boy! It is ees prride, Jacques. You mus' insiss that ee accep' somesing. An' every night I drream that ee is daid."

"I shall see him and find out how he is succeeding. I may be able to persuade him to take a vacation and come home to visit us."

"Ah-h-h!"

Madame cast herself against Jacques, and became as a fountain of tears upon his shoulder.

"You will have the small flat trunk brought down from the attic, maman. It needs a new lock. And you will see to the packing of my dress suit. I shall go to Boston, also, and I expect to call on Miss Sylvia and Miss Enid."

Jacques moved towards the door as he said this.

"Ah, that reminds me!" said madame eagerly. "I have a message. Wait, Jacques. You will want to hear. I have a message for you from Mademoiselle Félicie. She says" —

"Very well, later! At dinner it will do," he called from the stairs. "I cannot stop now."

CHAPTER II

JACQUES' BROTHER

JOCELIN had made that promise with perfect genuineness of desire and purity of intention. The difficulty with him was that he felt no responsibility about keeping it.

Sylvia said: —

"He holds a promise sacred. He has told me so, and his unwillingness to give his word lightly proves that. If I can persuade him to make me a promise, he will keep it."

She believed this to be true of him, partly because it was true of herself, and partly because he was such an admirable actor.

The keeping of promises had been a religious tradition in Sylvia's family for generations. When her ancestors broke faith, they either died at once or went crazy. But this had not been the case with the ancestors of Jocelin; for, instead of dying themselves, they usually fought a duel over the lie, and killed the other party. They were excellent swordsmen.

New York was not the place for Jocelin; it contained too much pleasure to the square inch.

His childlike temperament was too simple, too impressionable, to do aught save clutch at every fresh delight that came within its reach. The city was dull, as far as music was concerned, in August, September, and October, and he might have spent these first three months of his sojourn there in writing out Jeanne's music. He could not have explained why he did not do this, but the fact remained that it was not done. He knew he had promised to write those little songs, but the promise and the performance had no connection in his mind.

Curtis Baird had given him letters of introduction to various people who were likely to need music at their fashionable evenings or afternoons, and, by the middle of December, Jocelin had an engagement to sing at the house of one of these people during a reception. He arrived early, and charmed the hostess by his exquisite Southern manner, but unfortunately he was not asked to sing till rather late, and he spent the interval in the supper-room. He came to the piano with flaming eyes and a delightfully wicked smile. He tossed aside his roll of music, said he would play his own accompaniment, and, after one of his characteristically dreamy preludes, began a lively French song. He sang only the first stanza, because the son of the house happened to have heard that song before elsewhere, and knew what was coming next. Jocelin wanted to finish

it; he laughed obstinately in the face of the
young host, and tried to keep his hands on the
keys, but was finally persuaded to desist.

He obtained no more such engagements that
winter.

Madame sent her boy money from time to time,
and he earned a little for himself, spasmodically,
by singing in third-class theatres and music-halls.
His letters were vague and unsatisfactory, and in
the early summer he wrote that it would be safer
to address his mail to the general post-office, as he
was likely to change his lodgings often. After
this the letters came seldom, and madame no
longer showed them to Jacques and monsieur.

"Of course, if he won't come home, why, he
won't," Jacques said to his father. "But if he's
sick, we can't leave him up there to die. Mon
dieu, no!"

So, one cold Wednesday morning in December,
Jacques was loitering about the New York post-
office, making himself as inconspicuous as he
could under the circumstances, and keeping a
watchful eye upon the delivery window. He had
ascertained that his step-mother wrote to Jocelin
on Sundays, and he concluded that Jocelin, in
the hope of getting money, would come for the
letters with some promptness. He spent most of
the day near the post-office, but no Jocelin appeared. In the afternoon he hunted up the house
corresponding to his step-brother's last address,

and found it to be a crowded tenement with several families on each floor. After he had made many inquiries, a woman in the cellar volunteered a few remarks: —

"Did ee have a nose? Aw no! I ain't forgot that gent! He skipped out las' June. No pay! An' the ole Moriarty woman wot took 'im on trust, she went drunk t'ree days. Her mad was up high. Bad lot, wasn't ee? I know 'd they 'd be after him. Them Moriartys? I dunno. The ole man got the Island."

Fearing that he had been imprudent to leave the post-office, Jacques went back to it in the evening, but had no success; and it was not until Thursday afternoon that Jocelin walked up to the delivery window, received his letter, and slouched away. He was thin and bent, and he looked at no one.

Jacques followed him, not because he was ashamed to speak to him in the open street, but because he knew Jocelin's emotional possibilities, and did not care to precipitate a scene. He had no difficulty in following him unnoticed through the crowded, narrow streets, and at last, on a specially squalid block, the remarks of the juvenile populace began to indicate that Jocelin was near home. Two or three children greeted him with the words of a popular song, slightly altered: —

> "*Where* did you *get* that nose?
> Where *did* you get that nose?"

And one small boy, sitting on the doorstep of the house which Jocelin entered, said, in derisive tones: —

"Oh, no! he ain't no Jew! Look at dat beak! Oh, no!"

But Jocelin only shoved him aside, went in, and closed the door.

The house looked particularly quiet and unpleasant. The shutters were bowed or closed, and there was a dirty sign, "Room for Rent," in a window on the first floor. Jacques walked past and came back, and the small boy, observing him, cried: —

"'Ere y' are! This is yer place! Wark right up! She's expectin' yer!"

"Do you live here?" asked Jacques.

"Bet yer life I don't!" said the small boy. "Ho, ho!"

Jacques felt in his pocket suggestively. —

"Do you happen to know on which floor that young man lives who came in here just now?"

"Top," said the boy concisely. "He's de skirt-dancer's young man. Ain't he a bute?"

Then, looking down at the quarter which Jacques gave him, and back again knowingly at Jacques, —

"I say, does the guv'ment pay for this yer inquiry? On the quiet? Are yuh?"

"No," replied Jacques; "nothing of the sort. Are you sure it's the top floor?"

"Aw, who yuh bluffin'?" said the boy, still obstructing the doorway. "I bet yuh a quarter yuh take 'im off in de patrol!" And he held up Jacques' recent benefice.

"You'll lose your money if you do," said Jacques. "Run along; I'm in a hurry!" and he swung the young prodigal out of the way and entered the house.

On the second floor a door opened as he passed, and a woman's voice said:—

"Was it me you wanted to see?"

He answered, "No, madame," and continued up the stairs. Another man was coming down, and, by the light from the doorway below, Jacques saw that he was young and comparatively well-dressed. On the fourth floor there were three doors, and Jacques knocked upon one of them at random. Another opened, and an old woman poked her head out.

"Is there a young man, a Frenchman, living on this floor?" said Jacques.

"I guess so," she muttered, and pointed to the third door.

He knocked on this one, and, receiving no answer, opened it and stepped into the room, the head of the old woman remaining at the crack of her own door until he had disappeared.

Jocelin sat all hunched together in a rocking-chair by the window, and when he saw Jacques, he neither moved nor spoke. He seemed to have

outlived surprise and shame. He looked at his
step-brother as apathetically as if seeing him
were an every-day occurrence. There was a girl
lying across the untidy bed, and, when she realized that a man stood in the doorway, she sat up,
adjusting her hairpins, and said: —

"I told you some one knocked at that door."

The room was hazy with smoke and full of a
stale, evil smell. The floor was littered with
torn play-bills and ends of cigarettes. In the
midst of this grimy wretchedness Jacques' pros-
perity stood out arrogantly. Even he was aware
of it, and it oppressed him. That any one be-
longing to him should have been capable of falling so low filled him with wondering sorrow, and,
for the first time, Jocelin's weakness and incapa-
city seemed to be more misfortunes than faults.
There was neither anger nor severity in Jacques'
heart. He felt the uselessness of blame, of anything now save pity.

"Well?" he said.

"I cannot sing," said Jocelin. "My throat is
burnt out. My voice is dead."

And Jacques knew then that Jocelin's heart
was broken.

"I cannot sing," he repeated.

There was no despair in his words; despair is
active, and Jocelin had outlived activity. His
voice was dead.

Jacques' throat tightened and he said: "Never

mind! Never mind!'" in a lame, ineffective manner.

"Don't you believe him, now; he's only got a cold," said the girl on the bed, speaking in a soothing tone, and winking and making signs to instruct Jacques that he must humor the invalid, and acquiesce in this view of the case.

"Are you the skirt-dancer?" asked Jacques.

"I am that same," she answered, and she swung her legs nonchalantly against the side of the bed.

Her hair was blondined and all disheveled and dead-looking. Her face was thin and streaked with paint.

"I ain't *the* skirt-dancer. The four hundred ain't heard of me yet, but I'm gettin' there."

Jacques went over to the side of the bed and spoke to her in a low tone : —

"He seems to me a very sick man. How long has he been this way?"

"Pshaw! He's all right! He's like that when the opium's wearing off, that's all."

She answered with an assumption of bravado, but there was anxious questioning in her eyes as she looked at Jacques.

"How long has he been with you?"

"Six months, I guess. It ain't my fault!" she added bridling. "His voice wasn't no more than a squeak then. He'd 'a' went to hell a darned sight quicker if I hadn't took care of him!'"

Jacques stood near her for a few moments, thinking, and then crossed over to Jocelin. There was one other chair in the room, a rickety thing with no back; this he drew up beside his step-brother and sat down in it, laying his hand on Jocelin's knee to attract his attention.

"Tell me, Jocelin, how are you ill? Have you a cough?"

Jocelin looked at him vacantly for a moment, as if collecting his thoughts, and then he said: —

"I 've got everything — that 's bad."

"Don't you believe him! It ain't true," said the girl. There was a sob in her voice.

"Do you want to come home?" Jacques asked gently.

"I think I would rather die than do anything else," replied Jocelin listlessly.

"Who are you?" said the girl to Jacques. She left the bed and came to Jocelin.

"I am his brother."

She looked at him, turned her back, and walked over to the window. She leaned her arms, crossed, up against the dingy panes and pressed her forehead against them, and stayed there with her back to the two men.

"Get your hat, and come with me to a doctor," Jacques coaxed. "He will fix you up and get you in shape to travel, and then we will go home. Maman is waiting for you, Jocelin. She told me to beg you to come home. Never mind about

the work; when you are well again, we can think
about that. We will see what the doctor says,
and when you are ready to travel we will go.
Come! Get your hat! Where is it?"

Jocelin arose mechanically, and the girl by the
window whirled round.

"That's the way you do, is it?" she cried, in
a high, excited voice. "As soon as your fine
relations are ready to take you up, off you go!
What do you care about me? I'm nothing!"

"Where did I put my hat?" said Jocelin,
wandering bewildered about the room.

"I might 'a' knowed! I might 'a' knowed!
But I'm a born fool!"

While she raged and cried, Jacques watched
her gloomily. She loved this half-imbecile piece
of humanity that tottered up and down the room.
Women always loved Jocelin. There was that
singer-woman ten years ago. There was Sylvia
Bennett, — Jacques had always believed that she
had a liking for Jocelin at one time. He thought
of Enid, and he felt ill-used and alone. There
was injustice somewhere.

He did not remember Jeanne.

Jocelin finally picked up his hat, which had
been lying on the bed all the while, and Jacques
went up to the girl and held out his hand.

"I thank you for being kind to him. I believe
you have been, and his mother will be grateful.
If you care at all about him, you see how ill he

is, and how bad it is for him to be here. Please
take this for his mother's sake, because you were
good to him.''

He held out a roll of bills.

''I never did that yellin', and all that row, for
no money,'' she said sullenly. ''I'm fond of
him. He had little ways with him, soft and
quiet, and no more harm in him than a kid.
I'm goin' to miss lookin' after him. My Lord!''

She drew her hand across her eyes and turned
away.

''Still, I think you'd better take the money,''
said Jacques.

''Well, maybe I better had,'' she answered indifferently, and held out her hand.

He gave the money to her, and went towards
the door, where Jocelin already stood.

''Ain't you goin' to say good-by cat, dog, nor
nothin'?'' asked the girl.

''Tell her good-by!'' whispered Jacques, touching his step-brother.

''Good-by!'' said Jocelin.

They heard her sobbing as they went down the
stairs, at least Jacques heard her.

CHAPTER III

THAT same December, Sylvia's book was accepted.

She received the precious letter from the publishers in the noon mail, and Enid, coming home to luncheon at one o'clock, found her walking up and down the room, indulging at intervals in a short, delighted laugh. Beneath sorrow and weariness Sylvia grew painfully silent and still, but when joy came to her she found that she must move and speak, and she felt as if she were a stranger to herself.

She had had two or three little sketches and several short poems accepted during the year, and all the while she had been at work upon the book. Her tenacity of purpose filled Enid with wonderment. She was at work all the time, and working did her good. She seemed to dread being idle, to be afraid to stop one instant. The advantages of those years of vacillating effort, of writing and re-writing, of polishing and changing, showed themselves at once in her style. She did not have to waste time in getting command of her instrument. Now that she had something to say, she found herself ready to say it.

Her book was the story of a man who made a failure of his life. When she began to write it, she had not intended that he should fail, — he was an artist, not a singer, — but she grew interested in his development, and somehow she could not seem to make him do anything except fail. The book was unreal, illogical, otherwise, and Sylvia's appreciation of art made her at last consent that the hero should fail, rather than the book.

Enid read the story, chapter by chapter, as it was written, and found the young artist similar, in many respects, to Jocelin, but she did not say so. The plot, however, had nothing to do with Jocelin; that belonged entirely to Sylvia's imagination. The young artist was extremely dissipated, and, at the same time, devoted himself to painting scenes from the life of Christ, especially crucifixions. Worn out by excesses, he became insane, — imagined first that he was Satan, and had committed the unpardonable sin, and afterwards, by a sudden transition, became convinced that he was the Christ, and starved himself to death by trying to carry out the forty days' fast. It was a daring piece of work, and Sylvia felt desperate over it many times, but would not listen to Enid's pleadings that she should let such unhealthy speculation alone. The part of the book

that Enid found most incomprehensible was the
character-study of the heroine. She could understand why Sylvia should be able to portray the
artist, and why she should, by her very heredity,
be interested in morbid psychological investiga-
tion; but this heroine, this subtle combination of
intellect and sensuality, the artist's Magdalen, —
how could Sylvia understand such a creature, and
where had she ever seen her?

Sylvia only said: —

"She is real, then? You feel her?"

The publishers suggested modifications. They
felt that the English-speaking public was not
yet able to endure some of Sylvia's epithets, and
they could not quite consent to such a detailed
account of the second part of the insanity. They
thought that a treatment by suggestion would be
stronger; they feared that the majority of read-
ers might consider the present treatment rather
blasphemous. This idea astonished the devout
and reverent Sylvia, and she was convinced that
the publishers were mistaken in their judgment of
the public taste, but she agreed with them that
suggestion might be stronger than detailed de-
scription. The main point was that, with these
modifications, the book was accepted.

Enid came home to luncheon tired that day,
but when she saw Sylvia's face she forgot herself.

"Read it!" said Sylvia, thrusting the precious

letter into her hands, and, after a moment, in a
rapturous, wondering tone: —

"I have begun to be somebody!"

Her eyes filled with light.

It was Jocelin who had helped her to achieve
this success!

The thought startled her, and, frightened at
her own excitement, she turned and walked away
from Enid.

Poor Enid! who had dreamed once that when
this day came, Sylvia would say to her: —

"It is because of you. You have brought me
back to health. It is because I love you that I
have been able to do this. It is your help, your
encouragement, your faith in me, that have
brought me to a realization of my power."

She had known for a year that Sylvia would
never say this to her. She had schooled herself
to the knowledge that this was one of the things
she must do without, but she missed it now, because it had been a part of her dream of the happening.

After the night on the mountain-top, Sylvia
had said to her: —

"I have succeeded in making Mr. Castaigne
promise not to throw away his talents in future.
He is going to write and edit Jeanne's songs."

Enid waited for her to tell more, thinking: —

"After a while, when she has forgotten him a
little, when she realizes that her life and her

_work are more to her than any man, she will tell
me about it."

But Sylvia never told anything more, and Enid
knew it was because she had not "forgotten him
a little." And to-day, when her eyes were full
of smiling light, she had turned away from Enid.

They sat down to their luncheon with the letter
on the table between them, and they read snatches
of it aloud to each other between mouthfuls.

"How did your morning go?" asked Sylvia,
when they had arrived at crackers and New York
cream-cheese, and knew the contents of the letter
by heart.

Enid's expression changed.

"Do not let us talk about my morning," she
said, with a weary smile.

She was silent for some time, playing with her
napkin-ring, while Sylvia waited, gravely watching her.

Enid's face had lost its shining look of triumph
during the two years which had passed since her
winter in New Orleans. It was an older face
now, and grave, but more than ever interesting.
The beautiful lines of the mouth and chin expressed, even more strongly than they used to,
her high courage and faith and indomitable will,
but there was a new look in the eyes; they were
beginning to tell the story of renunciation.

The two years had been difficult ones. She
had been able to put her radical theories, to a

certain extent, into practice; she had been able to prove that, for herself at least, her social democracy was a practical and possible thing; but the elusive element called success, the uplifting consciousness of achievement, had gone out of her life, and she knew that, in the old delightful way, it was never coming back, for something in herself which had responded to it was gone also.

When she came back to Boston after her winter in the South, she found that she had ceased to be a novelty and an infant prodigy. The faddists had forgotten her and were running after new lions, — theosophic ones about this time. Interest in social and industrial questions had increased, but lecturers on those questions had also multiplied. She found the learned men, the pure scholars, in their same state of scientific inertia, weighing possibilities, perfecting definitions, seeking new points of view. Enid was a scholar, too; her mind rejoiced in dialectics, and dealt brilliantly with problem and theory; but there was something in her besides the scholar, something that warred with the scholarly impulse. She always wanted to put her theories into action, to see them working. She never waited to look at them from all their points of view. She told a very learned and uncertain man once that, if she waited to do this, she should do nothing else, as points of view belonged to the infinities of the

Creator. The learned man spoke of her after that as brilliant but not sound.

The great mass of ordinary, well-to-do, unintellectual humanity, absorbed in many and varied interests, found her singleness and constancy of purpose something of a bore.

The working-men, like their learned brethren, also distrusted her. They received her advances kindly, letting her know that they believed she meant well, but that they had no confidence in her judgment on practical issues. Her very scholarship and facility of speech proved a hindrance to her, for often those whom she wanted to convince and instruct could not follow her words, and did not know what she was talking about.

In the various settlements with which she allied herself she was cordially welcomed. Among individuals she made many personal friends, who adored her and told her all their sorrows; but it is a little wearisome to listen eternally to the other person's grievance, and there were days when Enid cried out against this constant demand for sympathy.

In her better moods, she realized and acknowledged that the giving was not all on her side, and she was grateful for the help which she received from these friends, — the silent lessons in patience, endurance, self-sacrifice, cheerfulness, — the training, as Enid laughingly expressed it, in the use of words of one syllable.

"I am a better teacher than I used to be," she would say. "My Back Bay school girls understand their history and political economy as they never did before, and it is because my friends in the other part of the city are giving me a free normal course of instruction in the art of simple and accurate explanations."

But to-day she had had a discouraging experience. She played with the napkin-ring till the little maid, the daughter of the carpenter who lived on the floor below, came in and removed the dishes with a daintiness and dispatch which bespoke somebody's good training.

"Was it the strike?" asked Sylvia.

Enid nodded.

"They think I have deserted them. I could not make them understand. I could not hold them when I spoke to them. They were grim and unresponsive. Two or three of the ones who know me well came up afterwards, and the pathetic part of it was the way they tried to show they were sorry for me personally, although they felt I had not been fair to them. They made excuses for me to myself, and one of them cried and begged me not to mind. They say I advocated the strike at first. Oh, Sylvia! one girl said she never would have gone into it if it had not been for me. And yet I told them in the beginning how weak and new their organization was. It is all a muddle. There was a labor agitator at the meeting, one of the fierce, violent kind, and he had those poor, tired women almost in hysterics. He understood my position better than they did. He knew where I was right. But whenever I tried to corner him he would not argue, he would only burst forth in invective. And I understood his position, too. We fraternized on several points, but he would not let them give up the strike; and in the end, although I could see they were a little uncertain, they chose ⁓to follow him, not me. It was natural that they should. He is one of them; he has had to fight the same sort of oppression they are fighting now."

She got up with a little laugh and walked to the window.

"Nobody trusts me, Sylvia, — nobody tries to help, nobody cares," she said.

"Present company, etc., I suppose," Sylvia remarked, smiling and following her across the room.

"Oh, yes, of course," she answered, and stood still, looking down into the street.

The next moment she turned round suddenly; and her face was decidedly flushed.

"Mr. Dumarais is coming here to call," she announced, and the unusualness of her remark made the forced calmness of her tone absurd.

"How do you know?" cried Sylvia staring.

"Because he is on the other side of the street; I saw him, and he saw me."

Enid picked up her hat and jacket, walked rapidly to her own bedroom, which opened into the little parlor, went in and closed the door behind her with a hasty bang.

"I wonder if Jocelin is with him?" said Sylvia; and she sat down, pressing the publisher's letter against her eyes, because the room seemed to be turning round.

CHAPTER IV

JOCELIN, SAVIOR!

At first the New York physician made guarded
statements about Jocelin's inherited delicacy of
constitution, looking at Jacques curiously the
while, as if trying to discover, from the relation
between these two young men, just how far it was
prudent to be explicit. But when he gathered
from Jacques' manner that plain speaking was
expected of him, he said some very plain things
in language both medical and colloquial.

Jocelin sat still meanwhile, apparently hearing
but little that was said. The physician advised
keeping him in New York at a private hospital
for a couple of weeks. By that time rest, good
food, and freedom from temptation would have
put him in a better condition to travel, and his
appearance would be less of a shock to his mother.

This proposition suited Jacques, who had been
considering how he should go to Boston if he
must watch Jocelin every minute. So the matter
was arranged, and Jacques wrote a letter to his
step-mother, telling her that her boy was not

well, and the doctor said he must be taken care
of for some time. He warned her that Jocelin
must not be spoken to about his voice, but suggested that she might have the piano tuned.

Jocelin protested against the private room in
the hospital.

"I will not stay here!" he cried. "Where
are my cigarettes? I will not remain."

He wept and wrung his hands. He abused
Jacques. Finally he sat down sullenly, and the
look of hopelessness came back to his face. The
next time he spoke he seemed confused.

"You always have your own way," he said to
Jacques, as if he were seeking some lost connection of thought in his mind. "You do as you
like."

"You don't know," said Jacques, moodily.
"I don't have my own way as much as you think.
Stay here only a little while, till I come back,
and then we'll go home. Shake hands, Jocelin'
we'll turn over a new leaf, you and I, — eh, my
brother?"

And Jocelin wept and mumbled, but gave his
trembling hand obediently.

Then Jacques went to Boston to find Enid.
And her, also, he found in the slums. When he
began to notice that he was once more in narrow,
ill-smelling streets, with children everywhere
under his feet, the memory of Jocelin's barren,
smoke-filled room and the haggard skirt-dancer

came back to him with a wave of disgust, and he felt sick. Presently the thought occurred to him that Enid was down here in the midst of this wretchedness, and he grew angry, very angry indeed, — with Enid, it is to be supposed, since no one else could be held responsible for the choice of her present abode.

When he entered the court in which she lived, the "Blind Alley," as he apostrophized it, he could not but notice that, although dingy, it was, comparatively speaking, quiet and respectable. Several small children stared at him and impeded his steps, but said nothing. There were muslin curtains at the three windows on the second floor of one house, and, as Jacques considered them from the other side of the street, Enid appeared at the middle window. He had been in a bad temper a moment before, but at sight of her he forgot everything except that he had come to find her and she was here. He lifted his hat, smiled up at her, and crossed the street.

The carpenter's wife 'on the first floor said she'd "see," and returned after a few moments with the information that he might walk right up, "second floor, third door to the left."

Enid and Sylvia welcomed him cordially, and Enid felt herself blushing again when he shook hands with her. It was flattering that he had really come back as he said he should. He looked so well! so capable! His eyes were on a level with her own, and smiled at her with such a frank and wholesome delight that her color grew still rosier. His hair was already beginning to turn gray on the temples, and it gave him a rather distinguished appearance.

They sat down and beamed upon one another speechlessly for a moment, as people will who have not met for some time. Then Enid said, smiling: —

"Well, how do you like our little slum? Do you approve?"

"I approve of the inside, yes!" he answered, looking around at the pretty room with its many books and pictures, its cosy window-seat and cheerful wood-fire.

"You are incorrigible!" laughed Enid. "Will you make no other concessions?"

"I approve of the inhabitants of the room, minus some of their convictions," he said teasingly.

"I foresee a discussion," said Sylvia, "and I move we rule convictions out of the conversation until Mr. Dumarais has told us something about New Orleans. How is Mrs. Baird?"

"Oh, yes! how is Roma?" cried Enid. "Tell us about her. She writes, but her letters are so full of 'Curtis,' we never find out anything about herself. Curtis is an admirable young man, we all know that, but a little of him goes a long way in a letter."

Jacques laughed.

"Just as hard on us as she ever was, is n't she, Miss Sylvia?" he said, and proceeded to chatter merrily about Roma and her husband, about monsieur, madame, the old house, — about himself a little, in answer to their questions. And, of course, he had to hear of Sylvia's book, which information he received in the polite, unappreciative fashion of the unliterary man. Sylvia thought that when she mentioned the name of her publishers he must surely awaken to the fact that she had written something worth while, but, strange to say, the celebrated firm-name had apparently no meaning for this benighted young stock-broker. He only said "Ah!" vaguely, and made a tame little joke about numbering an author — no, he said authoress — among his friends. He seemed much more interested in trying to find out what Enid had been doing, but she gave him scant satisfaction about herself.

Sylvia arose after a while and went to a table near the door of her own room. Standing there, idly ruffling the pages of a magazine, she said: —

"And Mr. Jocelin? You have not told us anything about him. How is he?"

There was a short, expressive silence. Jacques had anticipated this question, and had decided that he might as well tell the plain truth.

"Perhaps the less said about Jocelin the better, mademoiselle," he replied briefly.

Enid turned towards Sylvia with a numb feeling. What was Jacques thinking about to say such a thing? What would Sylvia do? Sylvia was standing by the table waiting for Jacques to continue. She had not even changed color; her face was quietly sympathetic and expectant.

Enid had reckoned without Sylvia's pride.

"New York has been too much for him," Jacques resumed. "I always knew it would be, but they wouldn't listen to me. It was hardly his fault. He never had any moral stamina. He is all gone, every way. No good! Never will be any good!"

"His voice?" asked Sylvia, and her own voice did not tremble.

"He said to me, ' My voice is dead!' and, I give you my word, I felt as if it were a person that had died. He destroyed it, and now it is partly that thought which is killing him. Such a voice as he had, that boy! I remember, when he was little, how he used to sing and sing! He was never anything but voice all his life."

"He is ill, then?" said Sylvia, opening the door of her study.

Her calmness had disarmed Jacques, and he spoke now quite freely. Enid could have strangled him.

"Ill, — perhaps it would be better to say worn out. The doctor says it is a wonder that he has lasted this long. He began to go down as soon

as he went to New York. He is there now at
a hospital. I am going to take him home with
me. I am sorry to be the bearer of such sad
news, mademoiselle; you and Jocelin were always
such good friends."

"Yes," she said, "we were. It is indeed sad
news. How grieved his mother will be! I am
very sorry. Enid, I am going to my room for
a while, and I will leave you and Mr. Dumarais
to revive old times by fighting over your convictions. Perhaps I shall write to the publishers
to make an appointment with them. I believe
we decided it would be wise to accept the royalty
offer, rather than the other one, — did we not?"
The door closed behind her.

She shot the bolt softly, and sat down before
her flat desk in the middle of the room. At first
her most clearly defined feeling was one of dull
amazement at herself. Did she really not care?
- For a year and a half Sylvia had been im-
mersed in active, definite work; her mind and
intellect had been sternly bent to the accomplish-
ment of a certain task; and in the interval her
tormented and overtaxed emotional centres had
profited by their long rest. They no longer responded indiscriminately to hysteric excitations;
they had become, on the whole, more self-respect-
ing; and of this Sylvia was not conscious, having
tampered so little with them of late.

When the first dullness had lessened, she began

to be aware that the reason she ought to be sorry, the reason she wanted to be sorry, was because he had broken his promise; and gradually there stirred the realization that she had been of no use to him, that she had never helped him. The humiliating thought crept in upon her pride and awakened it, and, on a sudden, the self-control had broken down before a torrent of grief and shame.

She had believed that God had intrusted to her the saving of a soul. To her! Oh, folly! It was not true. It never had been true. This was a just punishment for her pride and vainglory. Who was she that she should presume to believe she had been elected to save a soul? She was not any use, after all. He had forgotten as soon as he went away from her. He was dying, Jacques said, dying because he had worn himself out. And she had thought she could save him!

She made no sound. She sat with her chin in her hands and her lips set, and the great tears rolled down her face unchecked through her fingers. She was aware of curious contradictions in her consciousness. She knew, now that the shock had come, that all these months she had been dreaming that some day he would come back to her and say, "I have conquered!" But she knew, too, that she had expected this failure, that she was not surprised. It was strange, but she had been believing both these incompatible things for more than a year, — that he would make himself worthy of her, and also that he would fail. It was only a half disappointment.

"I was so sure of myself for a while! I worked; I believed I was worth something to somebody, but it was not true. I knew he could not; I knew it all along. The man in the book could not. Oh, I wish I had made the man in the book conquer! I wish somebody had conquered! Jocelin! Jocelin!"

Her Puritan sense of individual responsibility would not allow her to excuse him altogether. She could not say, as some might have said: "It was not his fault; he could not help it!" She believed he could have made a choice, and she knew he only drifted. She thought of his eyes as he knelt on the rock in the moonlight and promised to take up his cross and endure and work. She heard his voice again, singing, as he had sung when he went down the mountain in the early morning. He was very young to be "all worn out," younger than she, — he was only twenty-eight. Perhaps another woman might have held him, might have lifted him. But she, Sylvia, was of no use. Perhaps, if she had married him, she might have lifted him. But this feminine fallacy merely glanced through her mind, — it is losing its hold upon the women of her generation. She knew that marriage would not have helped Jocelin. No, even remorse could

not sting her, and she wished that it might. If
only she had done him a wrong, she might hate
herself for his sake. But he had suffered no ill
from her.

Jacques said he was "no good;" he had begun
to go down as soon as he went to New York.
She spread out her hands before her, as if to keep
some one away. She remembered how he stumbled past her door Mardi Gras night. She remembered how he looked at her when they sat
alone together on the mountain.

Why had he ever lived? Why did God permit such a man to exist and to be loved? She
covered her face. A man who only drifted, down,
down! What had he done except sing, and wear
his voice out?

She clasped her hands on the desk, and stared
down at the papers and letters.

It was cruel to let him come into the world
just to wear himself out. What was he good
for? Something, surely?

The letter from the publishers lay on top of
the other papers, and it caught her eye. She
lifted it slowly, hesitatingly, a look almost of fear
coming into her face.

What was he good for? Three hours ago,
who said, "It is Jocelin who has made me what
I am, who has set free my power?" Did she
remember that, as she sat with the letter uplifted,
and the startled, pondering look in her eyes?

One evening, long ago, Jocelin had played little inconsequent melodies on the piano, and sung little whimsical songs, and she had said to herself, "The world is in a hurry, — let it go!" Before she met this man, she had never rested, never relaxed; she was always tired from trying to keep up with the hurrying world. He had beguiled her into stopping a moment to take breath, and she had caught hold of life. She had said to herself that evening, "I must help him to be something, — it does not matter about myself. I will give myself up. I must help him. I will!" And after that she had begun to grow stronger, to forget herself, and to have confidence, unconsciously, in her own judgment. She had begun to write.

Was it she who had been appointed a savior of souls? Or Jocelin?

They would say that he was never anything but voice, that he had never accomplished anything. And yet she owed her moral health to him.

There was another night when she had said that he must plead for her before the Judge. Yes! When he stood there, shamed and weak and stained with sin, should she not stand beside him and say, "For himself he cannot speak. Let him say a word for me. I am his success. Nobody knows but me. He himself does not know. I did not know, even I, until he left me alone. And then I said I would stand firm, that he might say he had done what he could. I have made a little success. It is not much, — but it belongs to him."

Were these the things that Sylvia thought? Who can tell?

Was it that she did not love him enough, or that she loved him too well, to loosen her grasp upon life?

There were no more tears, and her face grew calm and gentle. Perhaps she was doing what her race had always delighted in, — dogmatizing concerning the intentions of the Almighty? Be that as it may, it gave her peace.

After a while she prayed a strange prayer in a whisper : —

"Lord, when Thou dost bid Jocelin to stand forth at the Last Day, set Thou also my secret sins beside his open faults, in the light of Thy countenance, that all men may see."

Then she wrote a business letter to her publishers.

CHAPTER V

SYLVIA'S matter-of-fact parting speech astonished Enid, but was sufficiently reassuring to
allow her to think about her own affairs, and she
found herself somewhat disconcerted at being
thus abruptly left alone with Jacques. She wondered uneasily what would happen, but she might
have saved herself the trouble, for only the direct
and definite could happen where Jacques was
concerned.

"You see I have come back," he said.

She tried to smile as if this remark were a
mere commonplace, but with his frank eyes upon
her, and the unmistakable meaning in them, her
attempt was a failure.

"Tell me of your life," he continued. "What
have you done this year and a half? Has the
philanthropy prospered?"

"Please do not use that maudlin word ' philanthropy,' " she protested.

He laughed good-naturedly.

"Tell me about the things you have done," he

reiterated. "Pardon me if I use incorrect terms; I am Southern and unenlightened, you know!"

She gave him a lame, dispirited account of her days, of her many committees and classes. She recited perfunctorily the programme of the Labor Union to which she belonged. She told him about some of the people who lived in the little court. She even touched lightly upon industrial questions and her unfortunate position in the present strike. All that she said seemed to her flat; and she knew that to this young cotton-broker, accustomed to rapid action and decisive results, her tale of beginnings, of cautious experiments, of unfinished systems, and half-developed theories which might not prove their usefulness and efficiency for several generations, seemed a recital of useless efforts towards a fanciful Utopia.

She ended with as little enthusiasm as she had begun, and waited indifferently for him to speak.

He had been studying her face while she talked, as if he found something new there.

"Are you happy?" he asked, still scanning her curiously.

The question roused her, and she drew back her head and gazed at him with startled eyes, as if considering before she answered: —

"Yes, very happy!"

Her voice was quiet and assured.

He continued to watch her, and waited, as if

expecting her to think better of her reply, but she went on presently: —

"Happiness is not necessarily mirth and laughter and jokes, and ease and luxury, and " —

"And sympathy?" he added.

She winced, and was angry that he should have detected this flaw in her narrative.

"I have Sylvia!" she said proudly, and held her head very erect. But her lips quivered.

He lifted his eyebrows, and tapped one foot impatiently on the floor.

"And Mademoiselle Sylvia, — has she the same aversion to matrimony? If not, it would be unfortunate."

Enid gave him a glance that ought to have annihilated him on the spot, and, turning her head away to the window, did not deign to reply.

He got up then and came and stood beside her chair, looking down, his hands in his pockets.

"You think I do not care for the things you care for," he said wistfully. "But that is not true. If I tease sometimes, that does not mean that I care for you less deeply. These are very beautiful theories that you have. They are noble, like you. If I cannot see always that they are practical, that is partly because I have lived a long time in the world of action, and I know that, if you don't down the world, the world will down you. It is an ugly thing to know, yes! Your way ought to be the true way, — your beautiful dream. But — experience makes me skeptical. Nevertheless, I should like to help you. I will never laugh, and when you are tired, — I think you are tired sometimes, — and when your people are ungrateful and the theory is slow in working, I will — I will " —

His voice was full of pleading, and, instead of finishing his sentence, he laid one hand gently on her shoulder, but she turned such troubled eyes on him he took the hand away again and put it back in his pocket.

"I believe in you!" he said. "I will stand by you in all that you do. You shall teach me to understand. You shall make friends with all the little shop people in French-town. We will give them afternoon teas and let them bring their children. Why not there as well as here? Listen! You are generous, you are reasonable. I cannot see that, under the present industrial system, I conduct my business other than as an honorable man. It is considered a legitimate business. Moreover, I have a family to take care of, — a father, a mother, and now Jocelin, who will be more and more an expense until he dies. I have no right to give up my business for the sake of a chimera. What would become of those who are dependent upon me and who cannot work? Perhaps some day, who knows? — I might be able to retire. I am not greedy; I do not anticipate being all my life a stock-broker. I promise that

you shall not have the business to complain of
any longer than it will take me to lay by a com-
petence. I believe in you! It will not be difficult, therefore, to make me believe in your theories. Come down there, and teach us the efficacy
of that eight-hour day, and that trade union.
We do not work so rapidly on these lines; we
need some one to wake us up."

She did not move, and he could not see her
face, but her silence gave him courage.

"That old house is so quiet! There are no
voices in it all day long. Your heart would ache
if you could see how dull it is. My father is
lonely and maman frets. I come in at night to
dinner, and there are only memories of people to
greet me. And I live over all those days of our
Jeanne's winter. Do you remember them? And
you are everywhere. I speak to you again, and
quarrel with you, and read aloud from those thick
books. I want you! Come and make a home
for me! It is no home now; it is only a dingy
house where two old people live with a man who
is lonely. You shall do as you like with the
rooms. Come and make them look like this one,
— as if you lived in them. When the world and
your people hurt you, I will not hurt you; I will
believe in you. Give me the right to comfort
you!"

How low he spoke! And he waited, standing
beside her, for his answer.

Poor Enid! It was cruel to come to you then, when you were weary, and a few kind words made you hungry for more. Home had such a sweet sound! And he was an upright man, a good son.

"Go away! please go away!" she said tremulously.

"No!" he whispered. "No! Is not the year and a half enough? Have you not learned your world? I have waited so long! Do not send me away now! And oh, the dear eyes, the dear eyes! Who has brought that look into them?"

Her answer was a sob, just one long sob without any tears. She pressed her hands tightly together in her lap, and looked up at him while he spoke.

"I shall work all my life, so that you may never be sorry you came to me. I will not be impatient; I will not ask you to come at once. No; it is better to wait a few months. It will not be pleasant while Jocelin is there."

"Jocelin!"

· Thoughts began to race through Enid's mind. What was this she was doing? Jocelin!

"He is ill. In fact he is — a little touched in the upper story. He will be worse before the end, and I know maman will never be persuaded to put him anywhere else as long as he lives. No, I would not bring you there while he is in the house. I will be patient" —

"No, no! Hush!" she cried, standing up suddenly and waving him away. "You are mistaken! What are you saying? I do not want to! I never wanted to! I did not know what I was doing! I was tired, and you are a good friend, but I do not love you well enough — oh, no! not nearly well enough! Leave my people? My work? Leave Sylvia? Above all, I could not think of leaving Sylvia now."

She was so excited she forgot how plainly she spoke, but he was too disappointed to understand her allusion.

"For a moment, because I was tired, I thought I wanted your — your home. But I do not! Why, of course I do not, really! I am not domestic — the way some women are. I should n't like to keep house and sew and — and — sometimes I think I should, and — but it would bore me. I should hate it! Sylvia and I share the responsibility here, and the maid works faithfully. There are only a few rooms. We have time for our real work, but a wife would n't have. And, oh! I could n't be just a wife! I don't want to! Please go away! I have chosen my life and I love it. I do not mind the rebuffs and the distrust. With my best self I do not mind them. Believe me, my happiness lies this way, and I am very pleased in my life. I do not need your pity. Forgive me for having hurt you! Your love has made my life more full; it has crowned my womanhood. But even if I had consented to-day, I should have come to my senses to-morrow and broken my engagement. Oh!" she exclaimed, as the full meaning of her narrow escape burst upon her, "how dreadful it would have been if I had married you!"

The remark was not complimentary, and the expression on Jacques' face brought her back to a saving realization of her conduct.

"Go away now and find a woman who will be a better wife! I do not love you,— don't you see? Else — I might feel you needed me more than my work — or Sylvia."

When he had gone, she sat on the window-seat trembling nervously. Jocelin was dying, and Sylvia belonged to her. She need not be lonely any longer, at least not more lonely than many women. And her work! Oh, the thought of being deprived of that! With only his love in return, his love and his amiable domestic tyranny!

Her courage was coming back, and the reaction from her previous despondency had set in. She began to think vigorously and hopefully once more.

Sylvia found her sitting alone in the twilight.

"Mr. Dumarais has gone?"

"Yes, he said he would come in to-morrow and say good-by! He leaves by the night train."

They were silent, thinking each of her own trouble, till Enid said:—

"We shall have to be very good to each other the older we grow, — we two lonely old maids, — shan't we, Sylvia?"

Sylvia, put on her guard by the pathos in Enid's voice, and thinking of her own loneliness, moved away to the fire and replied: —

"We always are good to each other, — are n't we? At least you are good to me. You must not feel blue about that strike, Enid."

"Oh, I don't any more! Some day, Sylvia, I want to tell you something."

"Yes, dear!" Sylvia was gazing absently at the fire. She did not say "What is it?" nor "Why not tell me now?" She did not mean to be unsympathetic, but she had had a difficult afternoon.

CHAPTER VI

SYLVIA UNDERSTANDS

"I HAVE business which keeps me here till to-morrow," Jacques had said; "I will call in the afternoon and tell Miss Sylvia good-by."

And as he walked down the little court the day after his interview with Enid, he was burning with a desire to give "Miss Sylvia" a piece of his mind.

Fortune favored him, for he met Enid coming away from the tenement. She had a private class the next hour, and felt relieved at being able to say good-by to Jacques formally on the street. She said Sylvia was expecting him.

Jacques had never known Sylvia well. He had always thought her a trifle sentimental, and he was particularly scornful of sentimentality. Moreover, she had tolerated Jocelin, which argued a certain weakness in her, — at least in Jacques' opinion. He had always taken pains to be scrupulously, unfeelingly polite to her; wherefore Sylvia, who was sensitive, divined that he had some grudge against her, and wondered, when she thought about him, — which was not often, — what the reason for his dislike might be. He took for granted, knowing the close relation between the two women, that Sylvia was aware of his attitude towards Enid, and, although to a certain extent he resented this, he did not wholly disapprove, since it gave him an opportunity for a frankness of speech which, in his present injured frame of mind, he was loath to forego.

"What a pity!" said Sylvia genially, when she opened the door in answer to his knock; "Enid has just gone out! She will be so sorry to have missed you! But perhaps you can stay till she comes back?"

Jacques looked at her in grim silence, and inwardly anathematized the duplicity of woman.

"I met her in the street," he said solemnly, when he had passed into the room and divested himself of his overcoat.

"Ah, I am glad!" smiled Sylvia. "Take that other chair, Mr. Dumarais; you will find it more comfortable. Our little apartment was so essentially feminine after we furnished it that we bought the large armchair in order to give an air of masculine protection to the rooms. Father always flees to it as to a refuge when he comes to see us."

Jacques took the proffered chair with unsmiling dignity, and seated himself at one side of the fire opposite Sylvia, who had drawn up a rocking-chair and was busying herself with some embroidery.

"You are making Boston a flying visit, Mr. Dumarais," she said, with exasperating cheerfulness.

"I see no reason why I should remain longer," he answered bitterly. "The sooner I go, the pleasanter it will be for all parties."

She looked up from her work in surprise and waited for him to explain, but he had shut his lips together and was staring at her defiantly.

"I am sorry if your business here has not been successful," she ventured.

"Mademoiselle, I do not see the necessity for our keeping up a farcical pretense of ignorance concerning a situation with which we are both thoroughly acquainted," he said, with haughty incisiveness. "If I have not been successful, it is because your influence has proved too powerful against me. You fill her life, she says, so that she has no need of the other kind of love. It is a thing improbable, but she says it is true. Evidently I do not understand women. And she, she will not understand me when I try to explain the difference. You have a loyal friend, mademoiselle. I waited a long time, — a year and a half, — and life has not been easy for her. And you, whom she cares for, — have you tried to make it easier, as I wanted to do? But my waiting makes no difference; she says you need her, and that seems to be sufficient."

He had risen, and his next words were stern: —

"Do you also be loyal! for I say that the time is not far off — look in her eyes and see ! — when she shall need, not you, not you, the woman friend alone,. but husband and little children. See that you be all these to her then! If you can ! Yes, if you can ! For, when that day comes, and she has not her need, I do not know in whose heart will lie the deepest bitterness, in hers, or mine, or yours !"

For the moment, Sylvia was startled out of all power of speech. Her lips moved, but no sound came from them. She could only motion to him to be seated.

He sat down again, as if it made little difference to him what he did, and contemplated the fire moodily, waiting for her to speak. Poor Sylvia! her whirling thoughts made her dizzy. She remembered so many things now which she had not taken the trouble to understand before.

A year and a half ago!

Her throat contracted so that she gave a little gasp, and Jacques, thinking she meant to speak, lifted his head, but her eyes were looking at him appealingly through tears; he saw she could not trust her voice, and he lowered his eyes without comment. Did not he suffer also?

"I must say something to stop this silence!" she thought nervously.

There was much that she did not understand, — and he thought Enid had told her all about it.

She would wait and find out, but now she could set him straight about one fact: he was under a queer misapprehension concerning Enid's motive for refusing him.

"Mr. Dumarais" (her low musical voice trembled at first), — "Mr. Dumarais, you make a grievous mistake when you say that Enid does not marry because of me. Indeed, indeed you do! And, for Enid's sake, I cannot let you go away harboring such a thought of her. All individuals hold a second place with Enid, because of her work. This has been true ever since I have known her. Even when we were young girls together in college, theories, humanity, came first with her, and personal friends second. I used to rebel against the preoccupation then, the apparent indifference with which she sacrificed her friends to her work. But now I — I" — Sylvia faltered here, uncomfortably aware of one of the reasons for no longer rebelling — "but now I am older, and I know that I honor her more than I ever did before. And I believe that her way of life is right — for her. I wish there were more of us who could set aside our own selfish sorrows, as she sets aside hers, and lose ourselves in the needs of other people."

"She said you needed her," repeated Jacques stubbornly. "Her work! — I do not quarrel with her work! I have told her that she shall do it just as she always has."

"But she couldn't!" Sylvia interrupted. "A married woman has other duties. Enid is free now; even her teaching, by which she earns her living, is along the same line with her social and industrial work. You think it is my fault. You will not be convinced, and I am sorry, but indeed I am not to blame. If she had to choose between giving me up and carrying out her theories, she would give me up, and I would wish it so."

"Oh, yes! I am not denying that you could give her up," said Jacques.

She colored.

"You are cruel, Mr. Dumarais! It is true that I do not love her as she deserves to be loved, but perhaps you do not either. She is worthy of a very great love; no one knows that better than I. I thank you for confiding in me to-day; I thank you for rousing me to a sense of my duty, and to a knowledge of how dearly I do love her, —for you have done that. And, for the other things you said, do not imagine that a woman, every woman, who elects to remain unmarried, does not take those things into consideration when she makes her choice. We are not young girls, Enid and I; we understand what we give up as well as what we gain. Do not be afraid of that! Believe me, I have not tried to come between you. Do not be angry, Mr. Dumarais! There are not many women like her; she cannot belong just to you, or just to me; she must belong to the world."

He was standing up again as he said: —

"Mademoiselle, you can understand, perhaps, that I am not in a mood to look at things from a gay point of view; therefore pardon me if I seem to you ungracious. I come here and I find her working for people who do not understand, in the face of adverse criticism. I find her weary; I find her — more beautiful than ever. And I would shelter her; I would give her a home, and money, and sympathy. But she says — you need her."

"If she loved you, she might realize that yours was the greater need, Mr. Dumarais!"

Enid herself had told him that, and he knew it was true.

"But," Sylvia reiterated, "it is her work that stands between you and her; it is not I."

And still he shook his head obstinately. But he apologized for any seeming rudeness of which he might have been guilty.

"Poor fellow!" Sylvia thought, as she watched him hurrying down the bleak little court. "It would have been absurd for Enid to have married him. I wonder why he couldn't see it? He felt very much abused. But I know he is mistaken about her motive for not marrying. I know he is! With all their polish, what a naïve charm of childlike directness these Frenchmen have."

Her eyes grew sad, and she turned listlessly away from the window.

Enid prolonged her absence intentionally, but came home at last to a smiling and penitent Sylvia, who looked into her face and shook her gently, saying: —

"I'll overlook it this once; but the next time you rush off and leave me alone with your rejected lovers, I shall conclude that you have designs upon my life, and I shall depart by way of the fire-escape."

Enid blushed and stammered, but Sylvia put her arms around her and whispered: —

"He thought I knew all about it, and he told me it was my fault, and he lectured me on my duty. My dear, dear! I have been very, very, — ah! I hope I have not been cruel! I never meant to be. I was preoccupied, and self-centred, and " —

"I should like to know what he means by coming here and presuming to take you to task!" cried Enid, with considerable indignation.

"I told him he was mistaken, dear!" said Sylvia. "I told him it was not my fault. Your work kept you from marrying him. But he was unhappy, and I could not seem to convince him."

She was taking off Enid's hat and cloak now.

"He took it very hard, poor fellow! And he was amazingly frank with me."

She laid the cloak on a chair, and turned back to Enid.

"I did not tell him I did not know about it," she said, and the color rushed into her face; "I thought you would rather he did not know that. And, — besides, I suppose it was pride, but I could not. So I let him talk."

"Thank you, dear!" said Enid softly. And after a few minutes, during which they stood side by side before the fire without looking at each other, "I have always meant to tell you as soon as you were not too busy to listen. You know that, don't you?"

"Yes, I know. It was my fault. Yes" (very quietly), "you need not protest; it was my fault. Do you want to tell me now? I should like to hear."

Enid nodded, and they settled themselves for a talk, Sylvia in the great chair, and Enid on the hearth - rug with her arm across Sylvia's knee.

"I began to know how he felt on the night of Curtis Baird's dinner " —

Sylvia moved uneasily. She had made a little discovery herself that same night.

"We had a quarrel in the opera-box at the ball."

It was Enid's turn to shift her position now, remembering the cause of that quarrel. No, she must not say what it was about. Sylvia might feel forced to say things which she did not care to say.

"I think he had not realized it himself till then, and I did not let him see that I noticed the difference."

"It is strange," mused Sylvia, "but I always thought he was in love with Jeanne. I thought that was one of the reasons why we were all so sorry Jeanne died. Oh, poor little child!"

"She never found out," said Enid, "and he — well, no, I don't suppose I do know what he would have done. However, it doesn't matter now."

She leaned her head against Sylvia's knee, and was silent a few moments.

"It was on the mountain-top that he asked me to marry him. I tried to tell you that night, but you were too tired. And afterwards, when I had wanted to talk to you alone several times, you said ' perhaps there were some things we ought not to speak of even to each other.'"

"Oh!" cried Sylvia.

It was a sharp sound, full of pain, and she leaned down, her arms around Enid's neck, her face hidden in Enid's hair.

"I did not understand," she said. "I thought" —

But she did not go on to explain what she had thought. She changed the sentence.

"I was preoccupied."

"Yes, I hoped you would let me tell you some day."

"You refused him, then, Enid? Or was it only a postponement?"

"No, I refused him positively, but he was persistent, and said he should come back. I tried to tell him about my work and the life that I must lead, but you must know how difficult that was, when he was so completely out of touch. And at last, when he continued to be obstinate, I told him about you."

"About me?"

"Yes! That I had no need of him, because you shared my life as he could never share it. That you were first, and therefore he could not be first."

"Enid! Enid, dear!"

"Why, yes! You know you are more to me than he could ever be. We are congenial, we understand each other, but he and so many other men live in a different world from ours. Something more than mere proximity is necessary, in these days, to make men and women fall in love with each other; we are not as susceptible as we used to be."

"Of course I don't mean," she continued after a pause, addressing the fire and smiling suddenly, —"I don't mean that a common purpose and a common work are sufficient. There are a number of young men here who share my views and willingly coöperate with me. To be sure, they are most of them clergymen who don't intend to marry, but that doesn't make any difference; it would be so delightfully improper of me if I could fall in love with one of them, or even several, but I can't. The fact remains that you come first. You are my friend. I have so many friends, I cannot count them. And he, the impossible he, would have to be the first friend on the list, which cannot be, since that is your place."

She lowered her voice and added: —

"It is twelve years now — did you know it? — since we began to be friends."

Sylvia held her closer, and looked over her head into the fire, saying nothing.

"How I used to build air-castles when we were girls! Do you remember? I used to say we would work together, vindicating our theories of democracy and industrial economy, you by writing, I by living. And, lo! the dream is upon us, and we knew it not. The dream is going to last all our lives long now, Sylvia. Do you mind?"

"No!"

"We don't get up and laugh and dance because the dream has come true. But that must be because we think it would not be dignified to do so, as I am thirty and you are twenty-nine. Yes, doubtless that is the only reason."

She smiled and clasped her hands around her knees, still looking into the fire.

"When my mother was thirty, she had lived her life. I remember she said to me, and I was only ten, ' I have lived a long time, Enid, a long time.' She was very tired before she died. But to-day, when one is thirty, one has only begun to live, and the long time is all to be. I am not complaining, Sylvia; there will be results some day, — there are results now. It is the best kind of result to be the right woman in the right place, and that is what I am. And that is what you are, too. You will taste the thing that I have tasted, presently; men call it success, and it is very sweet."

"I know," said Sylvia. "Father will be so proud, and rather astonished, — not shocked, I hope. And Fred will be amused, but gratified. And Fred's wife will give me a luncheon, — what a trial that will be! And if the book is a success, a number of people will look at me curiously whenever I am introduced to them, and young, would-be authors will send me manuscripts to be criticised. And if it is a great success, perhaps I shall have friendly greetings from some of the really great people."

"You have an excellent imagination, my dear! but you need not take that lofty tone, for you will enjoy these things when they come, even if you do know them all beforehand."

"Yes, I know that, also!" said Sylvia.

"Can you carry your fancy a little farther and

picture us at seventy-five, wearing caps, your
literary style labeled old-fashioned, my convictions branded conservative by the rising generation?"

"Yes, that, too!" smiled Sylvia.

"When people begin to call me conservative,"
said Enid, "I shall know that I have accomplished something."

"Enid!" Sylvia said, speaking with effort,
"I told Mr. Dumarais that, if it came to giving
up your work or me, you would give me up.
Was not that true?" She did not like to say,
"I hope it is true."

"Yes!" Enid answered slowly, "because you
would always belong to me, in my heart. No
amount of giving up could prevent that. That
is one of the satisfactions of having a friend. I
do not seem too cold or transcendental, — do I,
dear? We need not discuss such a mournful subject. I am not put to the test of giving you up.
I am allowed to keep you and the work also. I
am very blessed in my life, and I told him so,
but he could not understand. Nevertheless, it
was finally settled yesterday. And, Sylvia, I am
going to confess something very wicked now, —
even though I have refused him, I can't help
taking a little satisfaction in the fact that he —
loved me. It means something to be loved by
such a good man. And, — no other man ever
found me interesting in that way before. I am

glad such a thoroughly fine and upright man should wish to marry me, even if I don't approve of his convictions."

She laughed a little over that last word, and Sylvia, thinking of her own lover, — the man in whose proposal of marriage there had been no honor, — felt cold, but forced a smile.

CHAPTER VII

A BOOK AND A BABY

SYLVIA'S book came out in the spring, and the "author's copies" arrived at the tenement one bright April day when the barren court was yellow with sunshine. The voices of children fluttered up through the open window all around Sylvia, where she knelt on the floor, with her precious books in a row on the window-seat before her. She had thrust Enid laughingly away from them, saying: —

"No, no! You must not see them yet! Not till I have chosen yours."

And there she had knelt in silence ever since, touching the pretty volumes caressingly, putting now this one, now that one, at the head of the row, turning the pages deftly, as if she were handling velvet, or, with hands clasped, brooding above the entire collection, her face transformed by meditative wonder.

"It takes you an unconscionably long time to choose mine," laughed Enid from the depths of the arm-chair, which she had ostentatiously placed with its back to the window-seat. "Aren't they

all alike? I have a very interesting letter here
from Roma, and I am longing to read it to you;
but you have banished me from the books, and
now I do not even dare to seek solace in talking
of other things. The letter is extremely interesting, not to say exciting."

"Tell me about it," said Sylvia. "I can listen
and look at the books, too."

"I doubt it," returned Enid. "However, since
you insist, Jacques is reported engaged to one of
this season's débutantes, a Félicie somebody, — I
can't make out the last name."

Sylvia wheeled around suddenly, and, meeting
only the blank expanse of the back of the armchair, arose and went and leaned over the top of
it. Enid looked up backwards, and smiled reassuringly.

"Roma says she cannot vouch for the truth of
this, as she herself has not been going out this
winter; but Curtis thinks there is some founda-
tion for it, although he does not believe it has
gone to the length of an engagement. There are
two more pages about what Curtis thinks. Shall
we skip that for the present? They don't bear
very pertinently upon the subject in hand. You
can read them to yourself afterwards, if you
like."

"Enid," — Sylvia had come around to the side
of the chair, — "you are sure you are not sorry?"

"That Jacques is perhaps engaged?"

"Yes!"

"No, dear!" Enid spoke softly, and there was great sweetness in her clear eyes as she lifted them. "No, dear! I knew he would marry, — did n't you? I shall be glad when he does. The world's sons need to be fathered by just such vigorous, straightforward, healthy minded and bodied men. Of course, if he had remained unmarried for my sake, I should have felt honored, humbled, too, by such devotion; but even Dante, in his adoration for Beatrice, you remember, did not go to such lengths of abstinence as that. Men don't. To me, it does not argue inconstancy."

"I wonder," Sylvia murmured, "if she is like you? This other girl, I mean."

"No!" said Enid, with sudden emphasis.

The color came into her face, and she lifted her head with a quick, proud little motion.

"He would not do that! She will not be like me."

And then, more gently: —

"I think she is probably like Jeanne. And he will love her dearly, remembering Jeanne, and he will be very good to her."

Sylvia sat down on the arm of the chair and drew Enid to her.

"I am going to put you in my next book, — did you know it?" she said.

"Oh, no!" smiled Enid, shaking her head.

"I should not go well in a book; I'm too old, and there's nothing romantic about me; I'm stodgy."

"I know better!" Sylvia contradicted her, and, after a pause, mischievously, "Shall I make you marry him — in the book?"

"Yes, if you like! It would be quite as true to life as the other way, and the public are more used to it. But some times, Sylvia, I don't marry, — even in books."

They did not say anything for a while, but at last Sylvia broke the silence.

"Was that the only news in Roma's letter?"

"No! Let me see! Oh, yes! She says it is only a question of a short time with poor Jocelin."

It was always Enid, not Sylvia, who appeared embarrassed at the mention of Jocelin's name.

"She says no one sees him now but his mother and a man-nurse whom Jacques has kept all winter. It is the saddest thing I know of, that life."

"Anything else?" inquired Sylvia.

"Yes! The news with which the letter opens, but I have saved it till the end. Roma has a — little — girl!"

"Oh!"

"Guess what she is going to name her?"

"Jeanne?"

Enid's face fell.

"No! I never thought of that. I wonder why she did not name her Jeanne?"

"Dear little Jeanne!" said Sylvia. "And Roma was so fond of her! It hurts me to think that in a little while there will not be even the memory of her on earth. I wish that some one might bear her name and know her life."

"She's going to call the baby Enid, and she wants me to be its godmother," said Enid in a low tone.

"My dear! my dear! how lovely! I'm so happy!"

"So am I!" said Enid wistfully. "I can't help feeling glad to think there is one little life in the world which I have some claim upon, which I can do things for. I suppose I should feel very much bored and bothered if I had to take care of a baby every day, but, somehow, I'm glad this one will have my name. And she says such dear things about my having given her her highest ideal of what a woman ought to be. Here, read it, if you like! It makes me blush. Still, I think I shall write and suggest Jeanne."

"You will do nothing of the kind," said Sylvia hastily. "It would not be polite. You need the comfort of that baby more than Jeanne does. I'd rather it should have your name. Perhaps Roma will have another one, and we can remind her of Jeanne then."

Sylvia had gone to the window-seat as she said

these words, and now she returned with a copy of the novel in her hand.

"You will have to be godmother to this child, too," she said shyly.

And Enid opened the book and gave a little cry.

It was dedicated to her.

CPSIA information can be obtained
at www.ICGtesting.com
Printed in the USA
LVHW051439040121
675649LV00024B/278